Phonics Practice Book

Grade 2

MidAmerica Nazarene University
Mabee Library
Olathe, KS

Harcourt School Publishers

Visit The Learning Site!
www.harcourtschool.com/storytown

MidAmerica Nazarene University
110391

LB1631 .S13 2008 2nd

Storytown. Grade 2, Phonics
practice
book

Copyright © by Harcourt, Inc.

All rights reserved. No part of this publication may be reproduced or transmitted in any form or by any means, electronic or mechanical, including photocopy, recording, or any information storage and retrieval system, without permission in writing from the publisher.

Requests for permission to make copies of any part of the work should be addressed to School Permissions and Copyrights, Harcourt, Inc., 6277 Sea Harbor Drive, Orlando, Florida 32887-6777. Fax: 407-345-2418.

STORYTOWN is a trademark of Harcourt, Inc. HARCOURT and the Harcourt Logos are trademarks of Harcourt, Inc. registered in the United States of America and/or other jurisdictions.

Printed in the United States of America

ISBN 10 0-15-358739-3

ISBN 13 978-0-15-358739-9

8 9 10   0982   15 14 13 12 11 10 09

If you have received these materials as examination copies free of charge, Harcourt School Publishers retains title to the materials and they may not be resold. Resale of examination copies is strictly prohibited and is illegal.

Possession of this publication in print format does not entitle users to convert this publication, or any portion of it, into electronic format.

Contents

Unit 3

Long Vowels, *R*-Controlled Vowels, Consonant Digraphs, Soft *c* and Soft *g*

Unit 4

Consonant Digraphs, Short Vowel, Vowel Diphthongs, *R*-Controlled Vowels

Unit 5

Vowel Diphthongs, *R*-Controlled Vowels

Unit 6

Vowel Variants, Long Vowel

Cut-Out Fold-Up Books

The word **cat** has the short **a** sound. The word **pig** has the short **i** sound. Write **a** or **i** to complete each picture name. Then trace the whole word.

cat   pig

1	2	3
p i n	f a n	w i g

4	5	6
m a p	h a nd	h a t

7	8	9
cl i p	p a th	cr i b

10	11	12
m a t	six	fl a g

© Harcourt

Name Karen

Look at the pictures. Write the picture names to complete the puzzles.

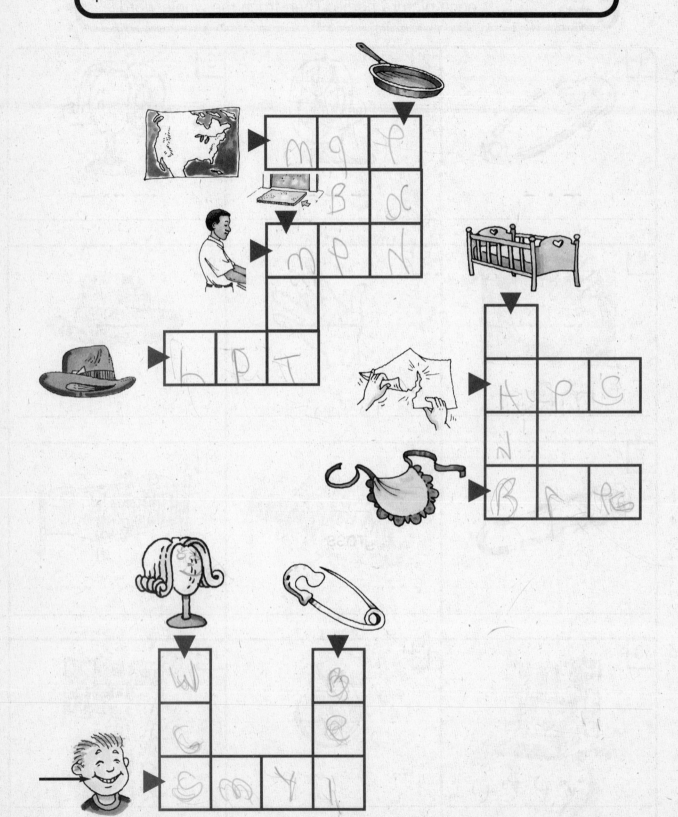

Short Vowel: / a / a, / i / i • Write Words

Phonics Practice Book

© Harcourt

Name _____

Write the word that makes each sentence tell about the picture.

| Sam | fit | hat | cat | is | big |

1		Sam _____ looking for his cat.
2		Sam asks his _____ sister Pam for help.
3		They look for the _____ in the yard.
4		_____ and Pam look in the grass.
5		Sam saw a _____ that was as big as a sack.
6		The cat _____ in the big hat.

© Harcourt

Short Vowels: / a / a/, / i / i • Read and Write Words

Name_____

cap	hit	bat	mitt
win	tag	ran	six

1. Rick used his new _____ at the game today.

2. Did you see the _____ Rick got?

3. I think Kim will make the catch with her
   _____.

4. Luke _____ very fast to the base.

5. Kim was able to _____ him.

6. Kim made _____ great catches today.

7. Luke's _____ fell off when he ran.

8. Who do you think will _____ the game?

Name _____

The **a** in **rap** and the **i** in **rip** stand for a short vowel sound.
These vowels are closed in by the two consonants, **r** and **p**.
When a word has only one vowel and the vowel is in the middle
of two consonants, the vowel is usually short.
Write **a** or **i** to complete each word with the short **a** or short **i**
sound. Then trace the word.

1 van	2 hat	3 l_d
4 p_n	5 flag	6 crab
7 map	8 cl_p	9 hand
10 bat	11 f_n	12 fan

CVC Pattern • Read and Write Words

Name _____

The picture names in each row rhyme. Write the word with the short **a** or short **i** sound that rhymes. Then write another rhyming word and draw a picture of it. Read all the words.

1.

dig

WeG

_____

2.

Nes

maP

_____

3.

Fen

Pen

_____

12

© Harcourt

Name _____

hen   fox

nut

The word **hen** has the short **e** sound.
The word **fox** has the short **o** sound.
The word **nut** has the short **u** sound.
Write **e**, **o**, or **u** to complete each picture
name with the short **e**, short **o**, or short **u**
sound. Then trace the whole word.

1. d o ck

2. b o x

3. l o ck

4. sh ll

5. t o b

6. b ll

7. t n

8. dr o m

9. s o n

10. fox

11. n st

12. m o p

© Harcourt

Name _____

1

sasserre

2

Tomans

3

Books

4

cacro lt

5

welte

6

Bell

7

Gaerare

8

Nete

9

Hage

© Harcourt

Name _____

Read the sentences and follow the directions.

1. Look for the jet. Color it red.

2. Sue has a pet. Put a box around it.

3. Find the bell. Color it blue.

4. Can you spot the hen? Draw a duck next to it.

5. Find the stem. Color it green.

6. Do you see the step? Put a big dot on it.

7. Find a net. Put a bug in it.

8. Find two men with a TV set. Color them.

© Harcourt

Name _____

Write the word that completes each riddle. Then read the sentence.

| hop | jet | bus | skunk |
| top | mug | bell | lock |

1. It is something that rings. It is a _____skunk_____.

2. It has four feet. Keep away from it. It is a _____.

3. It can spin round and round. It is a _____.

4. It is something you drink from. It is a _____.

5. You do this on one foot. You _____.

6. Some children ride this to school. It is a _____.

7. It can take you places. It is large. It is a _____.

8. It can keep you out. It is a _____.

Short Vowels: /e/ e, /o/ o, /u/ u • Read and Write Words

Phonics Practice Book

© Harcourt

Name _____

Add **s** to most words to tell about more than one.
Add **es** to words that end with **x**, **ss**, **zz**, **sh**, **ch**, **tch**.
Write **s** or **es** to make each picture tell about more than
one. Then trace the rest of the word and read it.

1 _____ pot

2 _____ glass

3 _____ box

4 _____ bug

Write the word that completes each sentence.

(**buzzes**   **dishes**   **hugs**)

5. Mom ___hugs___ her.

6. The fly ___dishes___ .

7. The ___buzzes___ are new.

© Harcourt

Name _____

Look at each picture and read the sentence. Circle the word that completes the sentence. Then write the word.

1	There are some _____ in the pond.	duck ducks duckes
2	They put dolls in the _____.	box boxs boxes
3	How many _____ do you see?	six sixs sixes
4	She found the _____ on the beach.	shell shells shelles
5	Her _____ are new.	sock socks sockes
6	Don't drop the _____!	dish dishs dishes

© Harcourt

Inflected Endings: -s and -es • Read and Write Words

Name _____

The letters **a-e** can stand for the long **a** sound.
The letters **i-e** can stand for the long **i** sound.
Write the letters **a-e** or **i-e** to complete each
picture name with the long **a** or long **i** sound.
Then trace the whole word.

c**a**k**e**

k**i**t**e**

1	2	3
r a k	v a s	b i k

4	5	6
sn a k	sl i d	wh y l

7	8	9
pr c	c g	h k

10	11	12
g t	n n	h v

© Harcourt

The letters **o-e** can stand for the long **o** sound.
The letters **u-e** can stand for the long **u** sound.
Write the letters **o-e** or **u-e** to complete each picture name with the long **o** or long **u** sound.
Then trace the whole word.

r**o**p**e**

m**u**l**e**

1	2	3
ros	ml	ct

4	5	6
hl	smk	cb

7	8	9
con	pl	hos

10	11	12
ben	glb	rb

Long Vowels: *a-e, i-e, o-e, u-e* • Write Words

Phonics Practice Book

© Harcourt

Name _____

Circle the long **a**, **i**, **o**, or **u** word in each question, and write it on the line. Then circle the answer to each question.

1. Do you see with your nose? _____Na_____ Yes (No)

2. Do you jump on a bike? _____No_____ Yes No

3. Do grapes dance? _____Yes_____ (Yes) No

4. Is a flame very hot? _____no_____ Yes (No)

5. Does a dog enjoy a bone? _____no_____ Yes (No)

6. Can a bird be in a cage? _____no_____ Yes (No)

7. Does a mule run fast? _____No_____ Yes (No)

8. Do mice run fast? _____no_____ Yes No

9. Is a fly huge? _____no_____ Yes No

10. Can a rose be red? _____Yes_____ (Yes) No

© Harcourt

Name _KAREN ROSO 5-17-00_

★ ★

Read the story, and circle the long **a**, **i**, **o**, or **u** words.

The Hike

Mike, Kate, and Mom sometimes go for a hike in the woods. They love to see the roses that are there. One time they saw a huge snake. It was not cute! Sometimes Mike and Kate play a game and try to name all the stones they see. They make up funny names. When they get home, everyone is tired.

★ ★

Now write the long **a**, **i**, **o**, or **u** word that completes each sentence.

1. Mike, Kate, and Mom walk a long way on their ___hike___ .

2. They like to see the pretty ___rose___ .

3. They don't think that the snake is ___snake___ .

4. Mike and Kate sometimes play a ___ro___ .

5. They make up funny ___rose___ for stones.

Long Vowels: *a-e, i-e, o-e, u-e* • Read and Write Words

Phonics Practice Book

© Harcourt

Words have syllables. There is one vowel sound in each syllable.
If a one-syllable word has two vowels, the first vowel stands for the long sound, and the second vowel is silent.
The **a-e** in **cake**, the **i-e** in **five**, the **o-e** in **hole**, and the **u-e** in **cube** all follow the CVCe pattern.
Write the words where they belong in the chart. Then write another word for each vowel sound.

dive	mule	globe	vase
broke	cane	ride	snake
slide	note	huge	tube

c<u>a</u>ke	f<u>i</u>ve	h<u>o</u>le	c<u>u</u>te

© Harcourt

Name _Karen Ro? 5-12-06_

Read each word. Add a silent vowel to write a word with a long vowel sound. Write the new word and read it. Then draw a picture for each new word.

1. cub   _cub_

2. tap   _tap_

3. not   _not_

4. tub   _TUb_

5. kit   _kit_

6. hid   _hid_

7. rob   _rob_

8. cap   _cap_

Name _Karen_ _Rojo_ _5-12-010_

Dean stops to fix his . When he is done, he eats a 🍑.
Color the pictures whose names have the sound you hear in
the middle of ⚙ and 🍑.

Long Vowels: *ee, ea* • Identify Words

© Harcourt

Name __Karen Rojo   5-12-010__

The letters **ee** can stand for the long **e** sound.
The letters **ea** can stand for the long **e** sound.
Write the letters **ee** or **ea** to complete each
picture name with the long **e** sound. Then trace
the whole word.

sheep

p<u>ea</u>ch

1 thre	**2** tre	**3** leef
4 j p	**5** seal	**6** beeko
7 bee	**8** reed	**9** wheel
10 team	**11** peael	**12** steam

26

Long Vowels: *ee, ea* • Write Words

Phonics Practice Book

© Harcourt

Name ___KAREN ROJOS_5-12-06___

1. Do you see a peach? Color it red.

2. Find the hat for a team. Color it green.

3. Add some meat for the man to eat.

4. Can you find a tea bag? Circle it.

5. Find the pot on the stove. Make steam over it.

6. Where will the woman sit? Make a seat for her.

7. Who will peel the peach? Put a bowl on her knee.

8. Who will sweep the rug? Circle his feet.

© Harcourt

Name _Karen Rose 5-12-010_

1. Do you put a hat on your feet? _No_   Yes   (No)

2. Is it wet at the beach? _Yes_   (Yes)   No

3. Does a hen have a beak? _Yes_   (Yes)   No

4. Does a leaf grow on a pig? _No_   Yes   (No)

5. Does a person drive a jeep? _No_   Yes   (No)

6. Does a sheet go on a bed? _No_   Yes   (No)

7. Is the water in a river deep? _Yes_   (Yes)   No

8. Can a seal run a mile? _No_   Yes   (No)

9. Can a dog have fleas? _No_   Yes   (No)

10. Is a scream a loud noise? _No_   Yes   No

Long Vowels: *ee, ea* • Read and Write Words   Phonics Practice Book

© Harcourt

Complete each sentence by adding **ed** or **ing** to the word in front of the sentence.

Clean ed   Jump ing

1. open   Jan _____ the door for her mom.

2. dream   Dan is _____ about the big game.

3. cheer   The fans _____ as the team came out
           to play.

4. ask   He _____ if he could go outside.

5. mix   Kate is _____ the food for dinner.

6. fill   Last week, they _____ three bags of
           toys to give away.

7. jump   The girls _____ higher than the boys.

8. fix   My dad enjoys _____ old homes.

9. need   She _____ to go to the store.

10. lock   My dad has _____ his car.

© Harcourt

Name __KATENRej l 5-12-010__

Add **ed** to the first group of words to tell what Lisa did yesterday.
Add **ing** to the next group of words to tell what Lisa is doing today.

walk

jump

kick

read

play

sing

____W9ik____

____j Ump____

____R ick____

____re9b____

____Y19Y____

____STnG____

Now draw a picture. Show something that you did yesterday.
Then draw something you might do today. Tell about your picture.

© Harcourt

Name _KAREN ROJO____4-28-06_____

Circle the letter that stands for the vowel sound in each picture name. Then write and read the word.

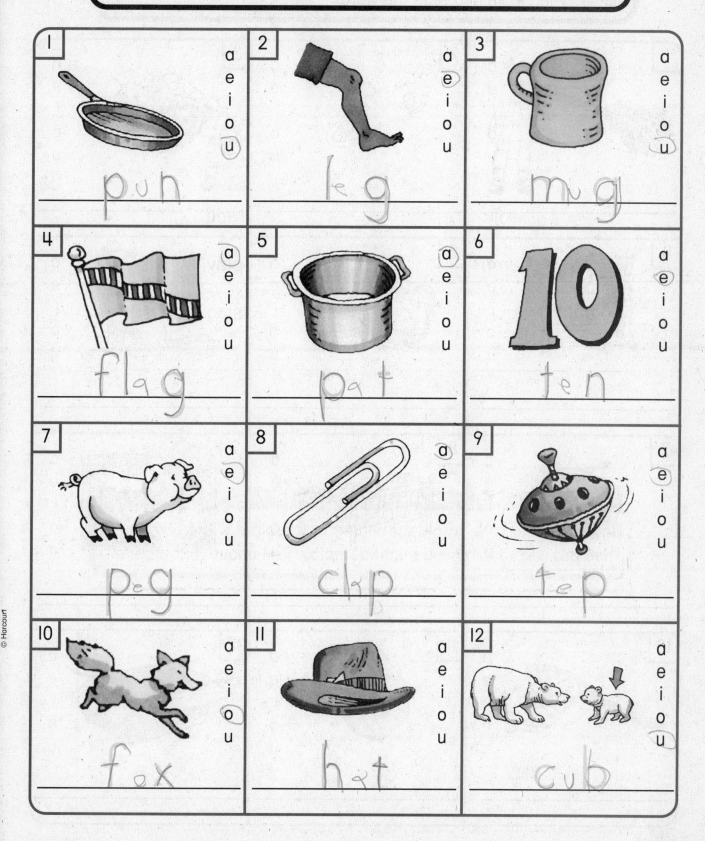

1. a e i o (u)   p u n
2. a e i o u   l e g
3. a e i o (u)   m u g
4. (a) e i o u   f l a g
5. (a) e i o u   p a t
6. a e i o u   t e n
7. a e i o u   p e g
8. a e i o u   c l a p
9. a e i o u   t e p
10. a e i o u   f o x
11. a e i o u   h a t
12. a e i o u   c u b

© Harcourt

Circle the letter that stands for the vowel sound in each picture name. Then write and read the word.

#	a e i o **u**	word
1	a e i o (u)	mleup
2	a (e) i o u	Pne
3	a e i o u	bielv
4	a e (i) o u	st pi replweße
5	a (e) i o u	selape
6	a e i o u	cat
7	a (e) i o u	crumse
8	(a) e i o u	curx
9	(a) e i o u	mare y
10	a (e) i o u	rete
11	a e i o u	sex
12	a e i (o) u	Box

Short Vowel Review • Read and Write Words

Phonics Practice Book

© Harcourt

Name _KAREN REJG 5-12-010_

Circle the word that names the picture.

1
sheep
steam
shape

2
mite
make
(mice)

3
bat
(bone)
bite

4
(tree)
three
tan

5
have
(hive)
hide

6
read
(red)
ripe

7
can
cone
(cane)

8
mile
(mule)
meat

9
hose
(huge)
hug

10
seal
steal
(sole)

11
bear
bay
(bell)

12
rock
reap
(rake)

13
cube
cab
(cub)

14
great
grate
(gate)

15
break
beak
(bake)

© Harcourt

Circle the sentence that tells about the picture.

1		I will take a beat. I will take a bite. I will take a bat.
2		The cube is melting. The cage is open. The cat is near.
3		The kite has stars. The kite is in the tree. The kite has a tear.
4		It is near a cat. It is a happy cub. It is very cute.
5		It will go on the pole. It will go onto the peel. It will go into a pot.
6		The boy went to the store. The boy went to sleep. The boy saw the sun.

© Harcourt

Name _K9r8N9oj0 4-28-016_

1
gone
get
(gate)

2
cat
cot
(cone)

3
(leaf)
leg
lane

4
teen
(ten)
tan

5
sand
steam
(snake)

6
hug
heap
(huge)

7
mile
male
(mule)

8
pine
(pin)
pan

9
steam
steel
(seem)

10
keep
kit
(kite)

11
(wheel)
while
whale

12
(tab)
tube
tub

© Harcourt

Name _____

Read each riddle. Circle and write the word that answers each riddle. Then read it.

1. They are on your legs. _____ feet   fat   fine

2. It keeps things together. _____ tap   tip   tape

3. You can sleep in it. _____ bed   bead   bad

4. You can drink from it. _____ cap   cup   cape

5. It means "very, very big." _____ huge   hug   hang

6. You can go places in it. _____ pan   plate   plane

7. You can stick yourself with it. _____ pile   pin   pole

8. A dog or cat may be one. _____ pet   pat   pit

9. You can put water in it. _____ tub   ton   tan

10. It may eat grass. _____ store   ship   sheep

© Harcourt

Short and Long Vowels Review • Read and Write Words   Phonics Practice Book

The letters **ie** can stand for the long **i** sound.
Write **ie** to complete each picture name that has the
long **i** sound. Then trace the whole word.

p**ie**

1	2	3
t	p s	b
4	5	6
fl s	dr s	cr
7	8	9
l	tr	t s

© Harcourt

Name _____

light

The letters **igh** often stand for the long **i** sound.
Circle the long **i** word in each sentence.

1. Beth slept in a tent last night.
2. She could hear an owl high up
   in a tree.
3. The sound it made gave her a fright.
4. It sounded as if the owl wanted to fight.
5. Beth turned on her light.
6. The owl took off in flight.

Write each word you circled. Circle the letters that stand for the long **i** sound. Then draw a picture for the word.

1	2	3
4	5	6

© Harcourt

38

Long Vowel: /i/ *ie, igh* • Read and Write Words

Name _____

Circle 8 long **i** words hidden in the puzzle. Some words go across. Some words go down.

```
N I G H T K T I E
K X K N I G H T F
D T L G G H I C L
R B I H H E N G I
I D G H T P L I E
E Y H T S I N M S
S K T I G E H C S
```

Write a word from the puzzle to name each picture.

1	2	3	4

5	6	7	8

Name _____

Write the word that best completes each sentence.

flight	tights	cries	night
pie	flies	light	lies

1

The boy _____ when he falls.

2

The two _____ landed on the cake.

3

It was cold last _____.

4

The dog _____ in the cool grass.

5

She wears _____ to keep warm.

6

With the _____, he could see the water.

7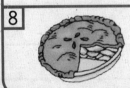

The _____ was on time.

8

Sam likes to eat _____.

© Harcourt

Long Vowel: /ī/ *ie, igh* • Read and Write Words

Name _____

In words that end with silent **e**, drop the **e** before adding **ed** or **ing**. Drop the silent **e** and add **ed** and **ing** to each root word. Write the new words.

They <u>live</u> in a house.

They <u>lived</u> in the house for three years.

They are still <u>living</u> there now.

1	hike	2	lace
	_____		_____
	_____		_____

3	save	4	bake
	_____		_____
	_____		_____

5	shave	6	tape
	_____		_____
	_____		_____

7	smoke	8	waste
	_____		_____
	_____		_____

© Harcourt

Inflected Endings: *-ed, -ing* • Drop Final *e*

Name _____

Base Word	-ed	-ing
bake	baked	baking
hope	hoped	hoping

1. The sun is _____ in the sky.
   rise

2. Outside, small animals are just _____ up.
   wake

3. I have always _____ mornings like this.
   love

4. Everybody walks around _____ .
   smile

5. My friend just _____ next door to me.
   move

6. Will and I were _____ our bikes at the beach.
   ride

7. We stopped and _____ in the water.
   wade

8. A fish jumped up and _____ us!
   surprise

© Harcourt

The letters **ai** can stand for the long **a** sound.
The letters **ay** can stand for the long **a** sound.
Write **ai** or **ay** to complete each picture name
that has the long **a** sound. Then trace the
whole word.

tr**ai**n

play

1 n__l	2 r__n	3 tr__
4 p__l	5 h__	6 ch__n
7 pl__	8 dr__n	9 s__l
10 d__	11 p__	12 sn__l

© Harcourt

Name _____

The picture names in each row rhyme. Write the rhyming words.
Then write another rhyming word. Draw a picture for it.

gray

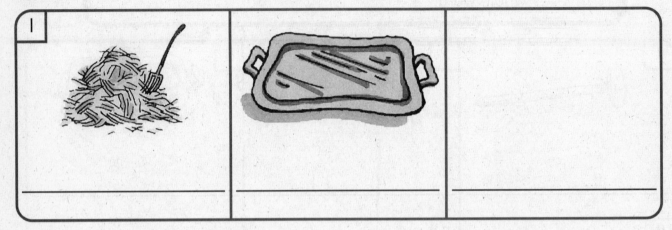

tail

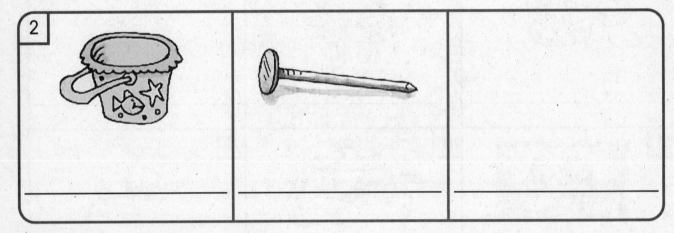

may

© Harcourt

Name _____

The letters **ai** and **ay** can stand for the long **a** sound. Read the story. Look for words that use these letters to stand for the long **a** sound. Underline them.

Jay and Fay sometimes sail on the bay with their mom and dad. The children put on life vests to stay out of danger. Sometimes the water in the bay is not steady. Other times, it may be mild.

"Today we would like to find some crayfish for dinner," say Fay and Jay. "If we had our way, we would go out in the boat every day!"

Write the long **a** word from the story that completes each sentence.

1. Jay and Fay like to _____.

2. They are in a boat on the _____.

3. Life vests help the children _____ out of danger.

4. The children want to find _____.

5. The children wish they could sail every _____.

Long Vowel: /ā/ ai, ay • Read and Write Words

© Harcourt

Name _____

Circle 10 long **a** words hidden in the puzzle. Some words go across. Some words go down.

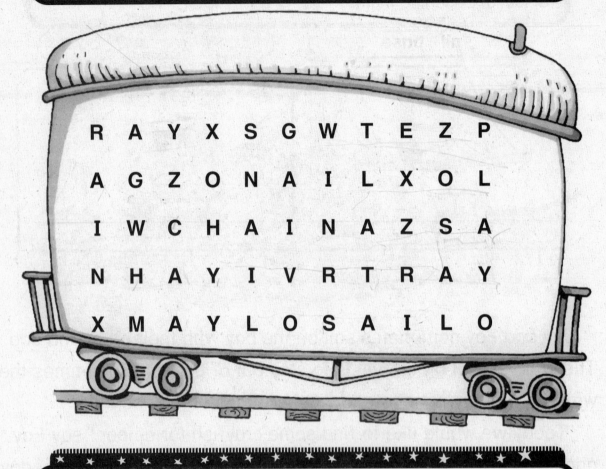

```
R A Y X S G W T E Z P
A G Z O N A I L X O L
I W C H A I N A Z S A
N H A Y I V R T R A Y
X M A Y L O S A I L O
```

Write a word from the puzzle to name each picture.

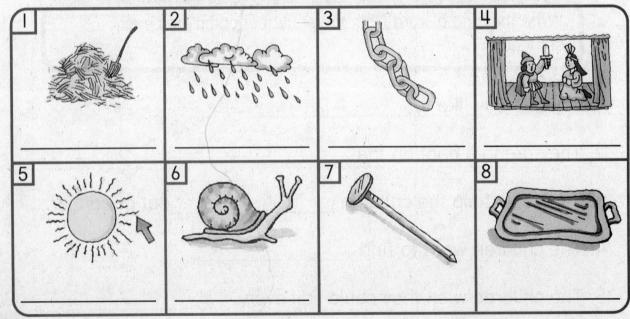

1. _____
2. _____
3. _____
4. _____

5. _____
6. _____
7. _____
8. _____

Long Vowel: / a / ai, ay • Read and Write Words

Phonics Practice Book

© Harcourt

Write the picture names. Use a word from the first box and a word from the second box to make each compound word. Read the words.

bath sail base side	ball walk tub boat

1 _____

2 _____

3 _____

4 _____

Put the word together to make a compound word. Write the word to complete the <u>sentence</u> about the picture.

5

Every + one

_____ is playing in the snow.

6

Every + thing

_____ is green.

MidAmerica Nazarene University
Mabee Library
Olathe, KS

Compound Words • Read and Write Words

© Harcourt

Name _____

Circle the two words that go together to make a compound word. Write the compound word to complete the sentence.

1		There is a lot of _____ in the spring.	shine slide sun
2		The boy and girl are standing _____ each other.	be bee side
3		The _____ is in front of the school.	flag pole pull
4		She loves to spend time on the water in her _____.	bat boat row
5	$3+1=4$ $4+2=6$ $6+3=9$	He did all his math _____.	home work with
6		She will be 10 on her next _____.	day bath birth

Compound Words • Read and Write Words

© Harcourt

Phonics Practice Book

The letters **ar** often stand for the vowel sound you hear in **arm**. Write **ar** to complete each picture name that has the same vowel sound as **arm**. Then trace the whole word.

arm

1. st __

2. b __ n

3. b __ t

4. c __ t

5. c __ p

6. sh __ k

7. f __ n

8. y __ n

9. j __

10. c __ d

11. sc __ f

12. p __ n

© Harcourt

Name _____

Write the word that best completes each sentence.

shark	barn	card	scarf
park	cart	yarn	jar

1 They like to play in the _____.

2 The _____ had hay for the cows to eat.

3 She used the _____ to make a vest.

4 Did you make your mom a _____?

5 The lid on that _____ is hard to get off.

6 The shopping _____ put a dent in our car.

7 That _____ must be one of the biggest in the ocean.

8 She wears a _____ in the winter.

© Harcourt

Name _____

1. Do you drive a card or a car?

   _____

2. Do you wear a star or a scarf?

   _____

3. Which sound does a dog make, a bark or a meow?

   _____

4. Do you send a get-well cart or card to someone who is sick?

   _____

5. Is it a jar or a jug?

   _____

6. Is it a sheep or a shark?

   _____

7. Does a farm have a boat or a barn?

   _____

© Harcourt

Name _____

yard	dark	large	started	farm
March	stars	far	barn	bark

1. It is very _____ at night.

2. I like to look at the sky to see the _____.

3. They are very _____ away.

4. Sometimes when I'm outside, I hear a dog

   _____.

5. The dog lives on the _____ next to ours.

6. The dog is very _____.

7. It sleeps in the hay inside a _____.

8. Once I slept in a tent in our _____.

9. It _____ to snow!

10. I'll never sleep outside in _____ again!

r-Controlled Vowels: *ar* • Read and Write Words   Phonics Practice Book

© Harcourt

Name _____

Most words that end in **le** have two syllables. Circle each picture whose name has two syllables.

1	2	3
4	5	6
7	8	9
10	11	12

© Harcourt

Syllable Patterns: Consonant -*le* • Write Words

Name _____

1	They put the food on the _____.	tumble table handle
2	That _____ is a good swimmer.	turtle candle marble
3	The _____ that has a lot of pieces to do is fun.	sample purple puzzle
4	Those _____ like to play in the park.	people purple sparkle
5	You should eat an _____ a day!	able apple handle
6	When the lights went out, we used the _____.	castle jingle candle

© Harcourt

Syllable Patterns: Consonant -le • Read and Write Words

Phonics Practice Book

Name _____

The letters **oa** can stand for the long **o** sound.
The letters **ow** can stand for the long **o** sound.
Write the letters **oa** or **ow** to complete each
picture name with the long **o** sound. Then
trace the whole word.

 boat

 bow

1	2	3
c____t	sn____	r____

4	5	6
s____p	cr____	g____t

7	8	9
gr____	t____d	sh____

10	11	12
c____ch	thr____	fl____t

© Harcourt

Name _____

The picture names in each row rhyme. Write the rhyming words.
Then write another rhyming word. Draw a picture for it.

grow

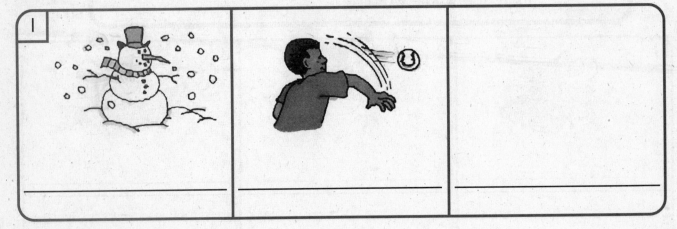

load

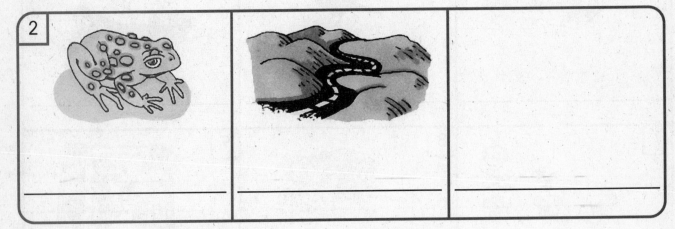

goat

Long Vowels: /ō/ *oa, ow* • Write Words

© Harcourt

Name _____

Circle the word that names the picture. Then write the word.

1
blew
blue
blow

_____

2
moan
mow
make

_____

3
soak
soap
snap

_____

4
bell
bowl
bone

_____

5
told
toad
toe

_____

6
read
rose
road

_____

7
show
snow
smoke

_____

8
flat
float
fold

_____

9
grow
groan
grate

_____

© Harcourt

Long Vowels: /ō/ oa, ow • Read and Write Words

Name _____

Circle and write the word that best completes each sentence.

1	At night I like to _____ in the tub.	_____	sold soak sock
2	I take a big bar of _____ with me.	_____	snow soup soap
3	I like to put a little _____ in the tub.	_____	bite boat blown
4	I watch it _____ in the water.	_____	float fold flat
5	Sometimes I try to _____ in the tub.	_____	robe row roar
6	But the water is too _____.	_____	lame lake low
7	At last I let the water _____ down the drain.	_____	flow flag fog
8	After a bath, I try not to look and feel like a _____.	_____	top toad tray

Long Vowels: /ō/ oa, ow • Read and Write Words

Name _____

Write the picture names. Use a word from the first box and a word from the second box to make each compound word. Read the words.

snow	row	tea	mail
post	pea	sun	dog

nut	pot	card	shine
box	flake	boat	house

1

_____

2

_____

3

_____

4

_____

5

_____

6

_____

7
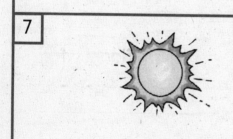
_____

8

_____

© Harcourt

Compound Words • Write Words

Name _____

sailboat	bedtime	fireplace	bathtub
seashell	paintbrush	backpack	sandbox
weekend	popcorn		

1. a brush you use for painting _____

2. a pack that goes on your back _____

3. the time you go to bed _____

4. a shell you find at the beach _____

5. a place in your house for a fire _____

6. a tub you use to take a bath _____

7. corn that you pop _____

8. the end of the week _____

9. a box that has sand _____

10. a boat with a sail _____

© Harcourt

Name _____

Look at the picture. Circle the word that best completes the sentence. Write it on the line.

1	We stay to play in the _____.	saw snow snack
2	There is an old rope across the _____.	trail train tell
3	The _____ rides in the boat!	get goat gate
4	The children like to play in the _____.	hay hog howl
5	The boat can _____ in the lake.	flown float flies
6	The _____ moved very slowly.	sack snake snail

© Harcourt

Name _____

1. Mother, ___
   we shop in here?   _____   may   me   my

2. We need a ___ to
   get to school.   _____   card   cart   car

3. I would like a ___ to
   lock my bike.   _____   chain   chin   cane

4. She likes to make
   figures out of ___.   _____   coat   core   clay

5. The animals live
   in a ___.   _____   barn   bug   bag

6. Do you see the ___
   on the tracks?   _____   tan   trot   train

7. It would be fun to ___
   with that.   _____   plan   play   please

8. This small boat has
   a blue ___.   _____   sail   sell   sat

9. She put the roses in
   a ___ vase.   _____   large   lane   lap

10. Before we go,
    I must ___ for it.   _____   pay   pony   pat

© Harcourt

Name _____

1. What rhymes with **might** and is the opposite of left?

   _____

2. What rhymes with **card** and means "not easy"?

   _____

3. What rhymes with **star** and is something you can ride in?

   _____

4. What rhymes with **darn** and is a place where animals sleep?

   _____

5. What rhymes with **tie** and is something you can eat?

   _____

6. What rhymes with **tight** and is the opposite of day?

   _____

7. What rhymes with **dries** and describes something you might do when you are sad?

© Harcourt

Name _____

```
S N I G H T R O L
O R O W I W S C I
A B H T G I O O G
P L E W H T A A H
K O L I E S K C T
R W F L I E S H O
L T H R O W H S C
```

Write a word from the puzzle to name each picture.

1	2	3	4

5	6	7	8

Long *i*, *o* Review • Read and Write Words

Phonics Practice Book

© Harcourt

Name _____

1. jam
   (jar)
   jeep

   _____

2. sill
   sole
   (sail)

   _____

3. light
   late
   (let)

   _____

4. bat
   (boat)
   bite

   _____

5. try
   (tray)
   tree

   _____

6. (grow)
   grain
   grand

   _____

7. dies
   (dries)
   days

   _____

8. knit
   (knight)
   kite

   _____

9. soapy
   (said)
   spied

   _____

10. pail
    pay
    (plight)

    _____

11. boar
    (bow)
    bay

    _____

12. pea
    pie
    (pay)

    _____

© Harcourt

Name _____

If I could Sail

If I could sail in a boat on the high seas,
I'd row as far as my arms would take me.
I'd hope to see a large gray whale,
But I'd stay *away* from a shark and its tail!

One day, I would lie inside my boat
On the waves I know I would float.
I'd watch as the crows take flight
And wait for night to see the stars' bright light.

1. What does the girl hope to see? _____

2. What does the girl plan
   to stay away from? _____

3. What does the
   girl hope to watch? _____

4. What does the girl
   plan to wait to see? _____

© Harcourt

Name _____

The letters **ch** stand for one sound. Usually they stand for the sound you hear at the beginning of **chick** or the end of **peach**. The letters **tch** stand for the sound at the end of **watch**. Write the word that names each picture.

chick

pea**ch**

wa**tch**

sandwich   patch   check   hatch   bench   chop

| 1 | 2 | 3 |
| 4 | 5 | 6 |

Circle and write the word that answers each question.

1. What do rubber
   bands do?   _____   such   stretch   chase

2. What do grapes
   come in?   _____   bunch   bench   brush

3. What part of
   your face is
   below your mouth?   _____   chain   chip   chin

4. What shows
   you the time?   _____   chick   chip   watch

© Harcourt

Name _____

The letters **sh** stand for one sound. Usually they stand for the sound you hear at the beginning of **sheep** or the end of **fish**. Write the word that names each picture.

sheep

fish

dish   shark   bush   shadow   shell   brush

Circle and write the word that answers each question.

1. What is a shark?   _____   bush   fish   chart

2. What is a loud sound?   _____   crash   crutch   class

3. What is a big boat called?   _____   sash   ship   sheep

4. What is something you find at the beach?   _____   shelf   sheep   shell

Consonant Digraphs: *sh* • Read and Write Words

Phonics Practice Book

© Harcourt

Name _____

The letters **th** stand for one sound. Usually they stand for the sound you hear at the beginning of **thimble** or the end of **north**. Write the word that names each picture.

__thimble__

nor**th**

| south | thumb | thermometer | bath | path | thorn |

1. _____

2. _____

3. _____

4. _____

5. _____

6. _____

Circle and write the word that answers each question.

1. What is March called? _____ worth   month   moth

2. What number comes _____ three   tree   thump
after two?

3. What is in between _____ fourth   sixth   third
fifth and seventh?

4. What do some flowers _____ truth   thumb   thorn
have that can hurt you?

Consonant Digraphs: *th* • Read and Write Words

© Harcourt

Name _____

Write the word that best completes each sentence.

trash	watch	path	bench	sandwich
children	catch	with	both	shirt

1. _____ my parents like to swim.

2. The _____ walked by the lake.

3. They saw a _____ on the path.

4. Trish was able to rest on the _____.

5. Dad was able to _____ three fish.

6. Bob's _____ smelled like it had been in the water.

7. Mom wanted to throw it in the _____.

8. Later, we each had a _____.

9. I filled my plate _____ lots of good food.

10. Then we went to _____ the boat races.

Consonant Digraphs: *ch, tch; sh; th* • Read and Write Words   Phonics Practice Book

© Harcourt

Name _____

Words are made up of syllables. Some words have two consonants between two vowels. To divide the word into syllables, divide between the first two consonants.

s i l - v e r

vc cv

Write each word, dividing it into syllables.

1 circus _____	2 pencil _____
3 picture _____	4 number _____
5 finger _____	6 chapter _____
7 sudden _____	8 bottom _____
9 balloon _____	10 picnic _____

Read each sentence. Write a word from above to complete the sentence.

1. The _____ of the basket had a hole.

2. He took a _____ of the entire group.

3. She likes to wear the jersey with the _____ 12.

4. All of a _____, it started to rain.

5. The first _____ in that book has many pictures.

6. Her _____ broke just as the test began.

© Harcourt

Name _____

1. She _____ the pretty dress.   looked   admired   completed

   _____

2. _____ dinner, everyone   worked   enter   after

   helped clear the table.

   _____

3. They saw a _____ at the zoo.   monkey   mistake   master

   _____

4. She caught her _____ in   flight   finger   football

   the car door.

   _____

5. The large ship was docked   harbor   number   homeless

   in the _____.

   _____

6. Have you _____ finished   apart   after   almost

   your homework?

   _____

7. She made sure to _____   invite   inject   inform

   everyone to her party.

   _____

8. Lily made a _____ on her   riddle   mistake   chapter

   science homework.

   _____

© Harcourt

Name _____

When the letter **y** or the letters **ey** are at the end of a two-syllable word, they usually stand for the long **e** sound. Write **y** or **ey** to complete each picture name. Then trace the whole word.

bab**y**

mone**y**

1 twent___	2 turk___	3 penn___
4 pon___	5 jell___	6 donk___
7 mon___	8 mank___	9 vall___
10 pupp___	11 hon___	12 fort___

© Harcourt

Name _____

The picture names in each row have the same ending as the word above each number. Write the words.

story

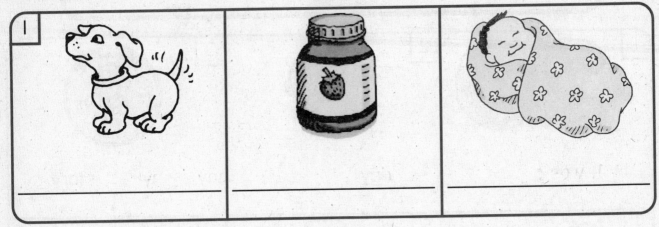

1 _____ _____ _____

trolley

2 _____ _____ _____

bunny

3 _____ _____ _____

Long Vowel: /ē/ ey, y • Write Words

© Harcourt

Name _____

1. It was a _____ day.

sunny   shy   story

2. I saw a _____ below.

very   valley   victory

3. I looked in the tree for some sweet _____ hoping the bees had left it.

homey   hay   honey

4. Instead I thought I would _____ an apple.

try   tray   they

5. I rested under the tree for _____ minutes.

forty   funny   family

6. I wished that I had some _____ to eat.

creamy   candy   country

7. Then I got very _____.

sleepy   sly   shy

8. I dreamed about a _____.

many   money   monkey

9. It was riding a brown _____.

donkey   duty   day

10. Later it got _____ so I went home.

way   wispy   windy

© Harcourt

Name _____

1. Is a chimney on a home? _____ Yes No

2. Is a cherry red? _____ Yes No

3. Does a donkey have two legs? _____ Yes No

4. Is the United States a country? _____ Yes No

5. Is honey sour? _____ Yes No

6. Can you count money? _____ Yes No

7. Can you eat jelly? _____ Yes No

8. Do you wash laundry? _____ Yes No

9. Does forty come before four? _____ Yes No

10. Does a horse ride a jockey? _____ Yes No

© Harcourt

Name _____

In many words that end with **y,** change the **y** to **i** before adding **-es** or **-ed.**
Add the ending to the word to complete each sentence. Then write the new word.

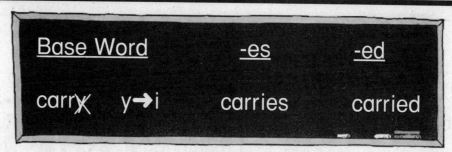

Base Word		-es	-ed
carry̶ y➜i		carries	carried

1. Alana _____ home.
   hurry + ed

2. She _____ a large box.
   carry + ed

3. There were soft _____ coming from it.
   cry + es

4. That's because there were _____ in it.
   puppy + es

5. In all, the _____ had eight legs and four ears.
   baby + es

6. Alana's friend _____ to use the clue to tell
   try + ed

   how many little dogs were in the box.

Draw a picture to show how many little dogs were in the box.

© Harcourt

Name _____

Look at the picture and read the first sentence. Then look at the second picture. Add **ed** or **es** to the underlined word to make a new word to fit the new sentence. Don't forget to change the **y** to **i** before you add the ending.

1

This <u>family</u> has four members.

These

_____

have six members.

2

This <u>baby</u> is happy.

These

_____

are happy.

3

He can <u>carry</u> the package home.

He _____

the package home.

4

She will <u>copy</u> the letters.

She _____

the letters.

5

The United States is a <u>country</u>.

The United States and Canada are

_____ .

© Harcourt

Inflected Endings: -ed, -es (y to i) • Read and Write Words

Phonics Practice Book

Name _____

When the letters **c** or **g** are followed by the letters **e**, **i**, or **y**, they often stand for the soft **c** sound as in **celery** or **slice** or the soft **g** sound as in **cage** or **gem**.
Write **c** if you hear the soft **c** sound or **g** if you hear the soft **g** sound. Then trace the whole word.

 celery

slice

 gem

 cage

1	2	3
___ ircle	___ iraffe	bad ___ e
4	5	6
fen ___ e	mi ___ e	ca ___ e
7	8	9
___ erbil	___ ycle	sta ___ e

© Harcourt

Name _____

Circle and write the word that completes each sentence.

1. They love to dance _____   stage   slice   sponge
   on the ____ .

2. The dancers practiced _____   trace   three   twice
   each dance ____ .

3. Each costume had _____   large   lace   hinge
   some ____ on it.

4. It cost fifty ____ for _____   cents   chance   cage
   a program.

5. People were also able _____   lake   large   lace
   to buy a ____ drink for
   one dollar.

6. The dancers formed _____   circle   cymbal   slice
   a ____ .

7. Some of the dancers _____   grains   gyms   gems
   had pretty ____ in
   their hair.

8. The show was ____ . _____   nice   nine   none

© Harcourt

Soft c and Soft g • Write Words

Name _____

Write the word from the box that completes each puzzle.

orange   city   giraffe   hedge
slice   circle   ice

1 A kind of bush is a _____.

2 A frozen form of water is _____.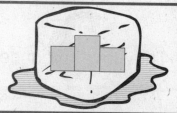

3 A _____ is a place with a lot of stores.

4 A round shape is called a _____.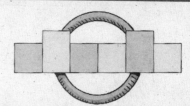

5 A juicy fruit is an _____.

6 A piece of something might be a _____.

7 An animal with a long neck is a _____.

Soft *c* and Soft *g* • Read and Write Words

© Harcourt

Name _____

Do what the sentences tell you to do.

1. Find the puppet stage. Put lace on the bottom of the stage.
2. Find the children in a circle. Put an **X** on the child in the center.
3. Find the table. Draw some oranges and orange slices on it.
4. Color the bridge blue.
5. The girl with a bow is eating some celery. Draw the celery.
6. Put a face on the giraffe.

82

Soft *c* and Soft *g* • Read and Write Words

Phonics Practice Book

© Harcourt

Name _____

In many words that end with a short vowel and a consonant, you double the consonant before adding **-ed** or **-ing**.
Choose the word that tells about each picture. Add **-ed** or **-ing**, and write the new word to complete the pair of sentences.

BASE WORD		-ED	-ING
HOP	+P	HOPPED	HOPPING
HUM	+M	HUMMED	HUMMING

set   hop   wag   nap   dig   scrub

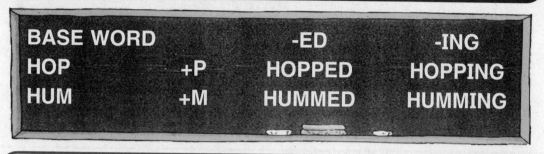

1. I make a big hole. I am

_____.

2. I got dirty. Mai Ling

_____

me.

3. I got tired and sleepy.

I _____.

4. Now I am playing. I am

_____

on two legs.

5. I liked playing. I

_____

my tail.

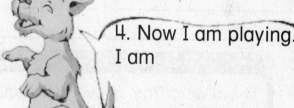

6. The day is over. The sun is

_____.

© Harcourt

Endings: *-ed, -ing* (Double Final Consonants) • Write Words

Name _____

Double the final consonant before adding **ed** and **ing** to each base word. Write the new words.

Yesterday   **Today**

chat

Yesterday, I **chatted** on the phone.   Today, I am **chatting** too!

1 rub	2 hum	3 plan
_____ _____	_____ _____	_____ _____
4 hop	5 clap	6 spot
_____ _____	_____ _____	_____ _____

Use a word from above to complete each sentence. You will not use all of the words.

7. After the show, everyone _____.

8. Her family was _____ a trip to the zoo.

9. After he fell, his mom _____ his foot.

10. The children were _____ the song.

© Harcourt

Endings: *-ed, -ing* (Double Final Consonants) • Write Words   Phonics Practice Book

Name _____

 The letters **er** and **ur** often stand for the vowel sound you hear in **fern** and **turtle**. Write the word that completes each sentence.

fern   **turtle**

curb	nurse	perch	germs	her
turns	surprised	fern	hurt	purse

1. My mom goes to _____ job every morning.

2. She puts everything she needs in her _____.

3. Then she walks out the door and _____ left.

4. She gets on the bus at the _____.

5. Mom takes care of children who are _____.

6. She helps children get rid of bad _____.

7. Every day I _____ on the steps and wait for

    Mom to come home.

8. Last Thursday, I gave her a pretty _____.

9. She was very _____.

10. What is my mom? She is a _____.

r-Controlled Vowels: *er, ur* • Write Words

© Harcourt

Name _____

The letters **ir** often stand for the vowel sound you hear in **bird**. Write **ir** to complete each word that has the same vowel sound as **bird**. Then trace the whole word.

b̲ir̲d

1	2	3
g___l	sk___t	w___g
4	**5**	**6**
cl___p	sh___t	___st
7	**8**	**9**
f___st	th___d	s___x
10	**11**	**12**
d___t	tw___ns	b___thday

© Harcourt

Name _____

The letters **ear** sometimes stand for the vowel sound you hear in **pearl**. Write the word that names each picture.

p<u>ear</u>l

| Earth | heard | early | pearls | learn | search |

1. _____

2. _____

3. _____

4. _____

5. _____

6. _____

Write the word from above that best completes each sentence about the pictures.

1. Elephant will _____ at school.

2. Elephant will _____ for Lion.

3. Elephant likes the _____ .

4. Elephant gets up _____ .

5. Elephant looks down to see _____ .

6. Elephant _____ her mom.

© Harcourt

Name _____

Choose the word that matches each clue. Then write the words to complete the puzzle.

| bird | burn | clerk | her | third | learn |
| dirt | search | shirt | stirs | turtle | whirl |

ACROSS
1. someone who works in a shop
4. something you put on
6. to look for
7. an animal that flies
8. first, second, ____
9. not him, but ____
10. something that soils your clothes

DOWN
2. to find out something
3. to turn very fast
5. a very slow animal
6. mixes
7. what hot fires do

© Harcourt

To divide a two-syllable word that has two consonants between two vowels, divide between the consonants.

bas - ket

vc   cv

Read each word. Circle the answer that shows the word correctly divided into syllables.

1. butter   but-ter   bu-tter   butt-er

2. almost   a-lmost   alm-ost   al-most

3. doctor   doct-or   doc-tor   do-ctor

4. finger   fin-ger   fi-nger   fing-er

5. number   numb-er   nu-mber   num-ber

6. plenty   plen-ty   ple-nty   pl-enty

7. mistake   mi-stake   mis-take   mista-ke

8. basket   bask-et   b-asket   bas-ket

9. forgive   for-give   fo-rgive   forg-ive

10. pancake   pan-cake   pa-ncake   panca-ke

© Harcourt

Syllable Pattern: VCCV • Write Words

Name _____

Read the story. Circle each word that has two consonants between two vowels. Then write each circled word on the lines below, dividing each word into syllables.

Today was class picture day. Almost everyone came to school in their favorite outfits. The first person I saw was Serena. She was wearing a silver dress with matching shoes. I admired her dress. Then Alexis entered the room. She looked like a princess! I must confess that I was amazed at how fancy we looked.

1. _____

2. _____

3. _____

4. _____

5. _____

6. _____

7. _____

8. _____

9. _____

10. _____

Syllable Pattern: VCCV • Read and Write Words

© Harcourt

Name _____

1. ship
   sheep
   shell

   _____

2. chick
   chip
   chair

   _____

3. press
   patch
   paint

   _____

4. bush
   booth
   brush

   _____

5. north
   month
   cloth

   _____

6. thick
   three
   thirty

   _____

7. branch
   bench
   booth

   _____

8. money
   more
   mint

   _____

9. bunk
   bunt
   bunny

   _____

10. cheery
    chimney
    chain

    _____

11. dolly
    dandy
    donkey

    _____

12. puppy
    penny
    pony

    _____

© Harcourt

Name _____

1. My dad always eats _____   lunch   late   lucky

  ____ at noon.

2. He has some ____ .   _____   track   turkey   tractor

3. He also eats ____ fruit.   _____   fried   fresh   fish

4. Dad puts ____ in   _____   hunt   handy   honey

  his tea.

5. Sometimes after lunch,   _____   sleepy   snore   sunny

  my dad gets very ____ .

6. But when he looks at   _____   way   want   watch

  his ____ , he knows

  he is late.

7. He ____ back to work.   _____   rushes   race   rinses

8. My dad ____ in with   _____   chips   checks   chest

  his boss.

9. They talk about the   _____   slip   ship   sink

  goods they have to ____ .

10. It costs a lot of ____   _____   many   money   matter

  to send them.

Review Consonant Digraphs: *ch, tch; sh, th*; Long Vowel *ey, y*
• Read and Write Words

© Harcourt

Name _____

Circle the word that names the picture. Then write the word on the line.

1	count cent send	2	cart circle square	3	skate skid skirt
	_____		_____		_____

4	gem gum grim	5	pinch purse prude	6	brook break bridge
	_____		_____		_____

7	lid lace lease	8	peels piles pearls	9	third turning turtle
	_____		_____		_____

10	fern feed feat	11	giraffe gopher goose	12	Early Earth Eerie
	_____		_____		_____

© Harcourt

Name _____

dirt	learn	gerbil	mice	third
hedge	since	herd	fur	turn

1. I am in the _____ grade.

2. Today my class will _____ about cats.

3. I will have a _____ to tell about my cat.

4. My cat has black _____.

5. She likes to chase after _____ with some

   other cats.

6. They look like a _____ of cats.

7. Once my cat chased a _____ .

8. It ran through a _____ and got away.

9. _____ that day my cat watches that spot.

10. He plays in the _____ and waits for the little

    animal to come back.

Review Soft *c* and soft *g*; *r*-Controlled Vowels: *ir, ur, er, ear*
• Read and Write Words

Phonics Practice Book

Name _____

Circle the word that names the picture. Then write the word on the line.

1	thrill chill shell	2	thorn torn wren	3	gopher gather giraffe
_____		_____		_____	
4	check wreck shock	5	cent cage hedge	6	sting steer stir
_____		_____		_____	
7	fern farm felt	8	mute many money	9	hatch hang honk
_____		_____		_____	
10	pear pearls pose	11	space slit slice	12	puppy penny party
_____		_____		_____	

© Harcourt

Name _____

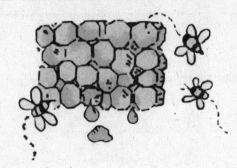
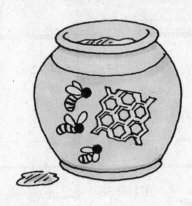

1. This rhymes with flirt and is something a person wears.   shirt   shark   dress

2. You do this when you look for something.   start   send   search

3. This is a drink made from apples.   cellar   cider   cycle

4. This is something a police officer wears.   bridge   brick   badge

5. These can make you sick.   germs   gems   gray

6. This is a story that you laugh at.   funny   fancy   fixed

7. You do this with a mitt.   crutch   cash   catch

8. An animal needs this to stay warm.   far   fern   fur

9. Bees make this.   sunny   honey   happy

© Harcourt

The letters **gh** and **ph** often stand for the sound you hear at the end of **laugh** and the beginning of **phone**. The letters **kn** and **wr** stand for the sound at the beginning of **knight** and **wren**.

Write **gh, ph, kn,** or **wr** to complete each picture name. Then trace the word.

laugh

phone

wren

knight

1 ___one	2 ele ___ant	3 ___ight
4 ___ist	5 ___ife	6 lau___
7 ___eath	8 ___cou	9 go___er
10 ___ee	11 ___oto	12 ___ench

Consonant Digraphs: *kn, wr, gh, ph* • Write Words

© Harcourt

Name _____

Do what the sentences tell you to do.

1. Make an **X** on the knight who is looking at the elephant shield.

2. Find the door with no knob. Put a knob on it.

3. Circle any letters of the alphabet that you see.

4. Add more flowers to the wreath.

5. Put an **H** on the horse that is in the wrong place.

6. Put a wren on the tree that the beaver is biting.

7. Put a watch around the king's wrist.

8. Put a box around each knife on the table.

9. Make a check mark on the rough road.

10. Write the letter **N** on the stall that is without a horse.

© Harcourt

Consonant Digraphs: *kn, wr, gh, ph* • **Read Words**

Phonics Practice Book

Circle 8 words with consonant digraphs hidden in the puzzle.
Some words go across. Some words go down.

```
G  R  A  P  H  Y  T  A  P
K  O  C  W  T  W  I  D  S
N  U  R  R  W  R  E  N  L
I  G  D  A  W  R  I  S  T
F  H  N  P  H  O  N  E  T
E  H  L  A  U  G  H  S  M
```

Write a word from the puzzle to name each picture.

1 Phone	2 Knife	3 laugh	4 Wrist
5 **Cat Names** Fluffy / Whiskers / Snowball graph	6	7	8

© Harcourt

Name _____

Write the word that answers each question.

knob	elephant	cough	wrong	dolphin
knife	enough	phone	write	photo

1. What animal lives in the water? _____

2. What do you do when you have a cold? _____

3. What do you do with a pencil or pen? _____

4. If you don't want any more,
   how much do you have? _____

5. What do you use to cut meat? _____

6. What is a picture you take called? _____

7. What are you if you are not right? _____

8. What do you turn to open a door? _____

9. What animal has a trunk? _____

10. What do you pick up when it rings? _____

© Harcourt

Consonant Digraphs: *kn, wr, gh, ph* • Read and Write Words

Name _____

The suffixes **ly** and **ness** can be added to the end of base words to change their meaning.

ly = in a certain way

ness = a condition of being

Replace the words below each sentence with a word that ends with **ly** or **ness**. Write the word.

1. Dad likes to cook, so he makes dinner _____.
                                    in a glad way

2. Dad chops the food _____ .
               in a careful way

3. He cleans up as he cooks because he likes _____.
                                          being neat

4. Sometimes his _____ means dinner will be late.
            being slow

5. Even the stew cooks _____ on the stove.
                in a slow way

6. Everyone comes to the table _____ when the stew is done.
                        in a quick way

7. It is with much _____ that we eat his great dinner.
          being cheerful

© Harcourt

Name _____

ly		ness	
1 slow _____		6 bright _____	
2 neat _____		7 ill _____	
3 quiet _____		8 kind _____	
4 brave _____		9 loud _____	
5 safe _____		10 neat _____	

Use some of the new words you made to complete the sentences.

11. She reached her house _____ just as the storm began.

12. The _____ of the thunder startled her.

13. She was awed by the _____ of the lightning.

14. She _____ waited for the storm to end.

15. Time passed _____ as she hoped the rain would stop.

Suffixes: -ly, -ness • Read and Write Words

Phonics Practice Book

© Harcourt

Name _____

The letters **ea** can stand for the short **e** sound. Write **ea** to complete each picture name that has the short **e** sound. Then trace the whole word.

head

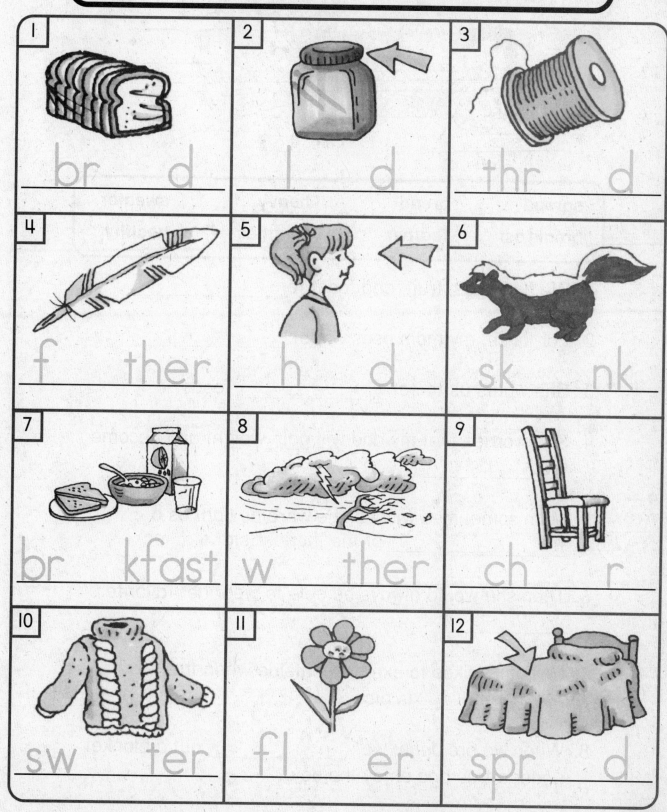

1. br___d
2. l___d
3. thr___d
4. f___ther
5. h___d
6. sk___nk
7. br___kfast
8. w___ther
9. ch___r
10. sw___ter
11. fl___er
12. spr___d

© Harcourt

Name _____

spread	bread	heavy	sweater
breakfast	feather	weather	healthy

1. We had eggs, fruit, and toast for _____.

2. For lunch, my mom uses wheat _____.

3. She wants us to eat _____ foods.

4. She worries that my dad will gain weight and become too _____.

5. Mom sometimes wishes she were as light as a _____.

6. Then she would always be able to wear her favorite _____.

7. My family likes to exercise outside when the _____ is nice.

8. When we are done, we _____ out a blanket under a tree and enjoy the day.

Short Vowel /e/ ea • Write Words

© Harcourt

Name _____

1		My cap is on my head. My cap is in my hand. I put my hand on my head.
2		He sees a pretty bud. He gets some books. He cuts the bread.
3		She sends the boy to bed. She puts a spread on the bed. She puts the jam on the bread.
4		It is so cold that I can see my breath. I am going to take a bath. Both of us like to play outside.
5		My father fed the hen. A frog hops to a feather. A feather fell from the hen.

© Harcourt

Name _____

1. Is bread cooked? _____ Yes No

2. Do you spread butter? _____ Yes No

3. Is thread something to
   eat? _____ Yes No

4. Is a sweater something
   that keeps you cold? _____ Yes No

5. Is breakfast a meal? _____ Yes No

6. Can you bury treasure? _____ Yes No

7. Is your head the lowest
   part of your body? _____ Yes No

8. Can you put a feather
   on a hat? _____ Yes No

9. Is a piece of paper
   heavy? _____ Yes No

10. Is rain a type of
    weather? _____ Yes No

Short Vowel /e/ ea • Read and Write Words

© Harcourt

Name _____

For two-syllable words that have a single consonant between two vowels, the word is usually divided before the consonant if the first vowel is long.

lady   **la - dy**

                  v   cv

Write each word, dividing it into syllables.

1 moment _____	2 polar _____
3 tiny _____	4 frozen _____
5 paper _____	6 lazy _____
7 pony _____	8 famous _____
9 sofa _____	10 spider _____

Read each sentence. Write a word from above to complete the sentence.

1. Have you ever seen a _____ bear?

2. They live in cold places where the ice is

   _____ .

3. These animals sleep a lot, but they are not

   _____ .

4. They are _____ for catching fish.

5. They wait for the perfect _____ to strike.

6. The _____ fish have no way to escape.

© Harcourt

Name _____

Circle and write the word to complete each sentence. Then write the word on the second line, dividing it into syllables.

1. Ken likes to listen to __ on the radio.

_____

_____

music   toys   noise

2. That __ is wearing a green sweater.

_____

_____

lion   lemon   lady

3. He drew on his homework __.

_____

_____

seat   paper   cage

4. Mark is the teacher's favorite __.

_____

_____

pupil   pilot   peach

5. He likes to eat __ yogurt.

_____

_____

feature   finish   frozen

6. She is a __ dancer.

_____

_____

fancy   famous   forty

7. My sister is scared of __.

_____

_____

spiders   spinning   scents

8. That __ is brown and white.

_____

_____

puny   pony   punt

Syllable Pattern: V/CV • Read and Write Words

Phonics Practice Book

© Harcourt

Name _____

b<u>oy</u>

p<u>oi</u>nt

The letters **oi** and **oy** usually stand for the vowel sound you hear in **point** and **boy**. Read the story. Then draw a picture to show what happens in the story. Use words from the story to label things in your picture.

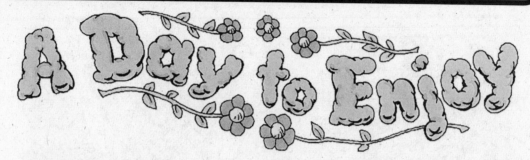

A Day to Enjoy

Hi, I'm Joy.

My name is Joy. I am a girl dog, not a boy dog. Today I dug a hole in the garden soil. First I found my lost toy. Then I found some coins. Today was a day I did enjoy!

Now circle all the words that have the vowel sound you hear in **point** and **boy**.

© Harcourt

Name _____

points	soil	cowboys	join
enjoy	noise	boiled	coiled

1. We _____ going on long rides on horses.

2. We make believe we are cowgirls and _____.

3. Once we heard a snake's loud _____.

4. We saw a snake in the dirt, or _____.

5. The snake was _____, so we rode away.

6. Another time, we rode to a place where two streams

   _____, or come together.

7. We camped near a big rock with five _____

   on it.

8. Then we _____ water over the hot campfire.

© Harcourt

Name _____

1		The boy spills a glass of water. The boy put it away so it would not spoil. The boy puts it in some soil.
2		Joy gets a toy for her birthday. Joy points to the tent. Joy finds a coin on her birthday.
3		She boils some soup in a pot. She puts water in a pot to boil. She fills the pot with soil.
4		Troy hears an owl. Troy puts oil on the sail. Troy has an oyster shell.
5		The toy drum is on the table. The drum makes a loud noise. The noise comes from the dogs.
6	10¢ ←	The dime has three points on it. The toy paints are mine. It points to the dime.

© Harcourt

Name _____

Circle and write the word that answers the riddle.

1. You sometimes
   play with me.   _____   boil   toy   enjoy

2. I can be a dime
   or a quarter.   _____   coil   foil   coin

3. I am at the end
   of a pencil.   _____   point   cowboy   oil

4. I mean "happy."   _____   boys   joyful   join

5. You can plant
   in me.   _____   snail   soy   soil

6. I am what a
   pig says.   _____   oink   oil   joy

7. I am what very
   hot water does.   _____   boils   bays   boys

8. I am a very
   loud sound.   _____   moist   noise   broil

9. I mean "not
   good anymore."   _____   spoiled   loyal   annoyed

Vowel Diphthong: / oi / *oi, oy* • Read and Write Words   Phonics Practice Book

© Harcourt

Name _____

The suffixes **ful** and **less** can be added to the end of base words to change their meaning.

ful = full of or enough to fill

less = without

Replace the words below each sentence with a word that ends with **ful** or **less**. Write the word.

1. When you hold a new baby, you must be _____.
   full of care

2. There might be many _____ nights when a baby first comes home.
   without sleep

3. There will be many _____ hours playing with the baby.
   full of joy

4. You can be _____ to new parents by playing with the baby.
   full of help

5. Since babies are _____ , they need others to feed them and dress them.
   without help

6. When a baby naps, be _____ by being quiet.
   full of thought

7. A new baby is a _____ addition to a family!
   full of wonder

© Harcourt

Name _____

Use **ful** or **less**. Write a word to match each definition.

1 without joy _____	2 full of cheer _____	3 full of thanks _____
4 without a care _____	5 without fear _____	6 full of hope _____
7 without taste _____	8 full of fear _____	9 without a tooth _____

Add **ful** or **less** to the base words to complete each phrase.

1. sleep_____ nights

2. cup_____ of sugar

3. sugar_____ gum

4. taste_____ water

5. joy_____ holiday

6. seed_____ grapes

Suffixes: -ful, -less • Write Words

Phonics Practice Book

© Harcourt

Name _____

deer The letters **eer** and **ear** sometimes stand for the vowel sound you hear in **deer** and **tear**.

tear Write the word that answers each riddle.

peer	fear	near	ears
cheer	hear	year	steer

1. You have two of me on your head. _____

2. I am 12 months long. _____

3. If you are afraid, you are full of me. _____

4. I am what you do when you listen. _____

5. I am what you do when you want
   your team to win. _____

6. I mean "not far." _____

7. I am what you do to make a bike
   go where you want it to. _____

8. I mean "to look at." _____

© Harcourt

Name _____

Circle the word that names the picture. Then write the word on the line.

1	spade spear shell	2	tar tail tear	3	deer dark door
4	gets goats gears	5	bear beard bored	6	ore ear are
7	year your yearn	8	chair cherry cheer	9	steer stair stare

r-Controlled Vowels: *ear, eer* • Write Words

Phonics Practice Book

© Harcourt

Name _____

Read each sentence and circle the word that has the vowel sound you hear in **deer** and **tear**.

1. A deer was in the meadow.

2. From where he stood, he could hear if someone came too close.

3. He liked to be near the stream.

4. At one time, hunters came with spears.

5. It had been many years since that happened.

6. Once a man with a beard came and took pictures.

Write each word you circled. Then draw a picture for it.

1	2	3

4	5	6

© Harcourt

Name _____

Circle and write the word that best completes each sentence.

1. On a _____ day, most people like to be outside.

_____ clerk clear clean

2. My mom often calls my dad _____.

_____ dare drain dear

3. My best friend lives _____ me.

_____ near need note

4. Everyone _____ at soccer games.

_____ cases cheers chairs

5. Have you ever seen a _____ in the meadow?

_____ deer darn dent

6. It took my brother a _____ to learn how to ride a bike.

_____ yard yarn year

7. She was able to _____ at the puppy in the pet store.

_____ pear peer peel

8. He had a pain in his left _____.

_____ ear end and

9. My dad used to have a _____.

_____ bend bead beard

10. Did you _____ that loud noise?

_____ hair hear heed

© Harcourt

r-Controlled Vowels: *ear, eer* • Read and Write Words

Name _____

For two-syllable words that have a single consonant between two vowels, the word is usually divided after the consonant if the first vowel is short.

model	mod - el
	vc v

Write each word, dividing it into syllables.

1. rivers _____	2. finish _____
3. clever _____	4. lemon _____
5. travel _____	6. ever _____
7. cabin _____	8. visit _____
9. figure _____	10. palace _____

Read each sentence. Write a word from above to complete the sentence.

1. Someday I hope to _____ faraway places.

2. I want to _____ across the world.

3. I would like to sail on deep _____.

4. Maybe I would live in a _____ in the woods.

5. It might not be a _____, but it would be a great home.

6. I'd be so _____ that I'd find food all around me.

© Harcourt

Name _____

1. He likes to have   _____   lasting   lender   lemon
   a slice of __ in
   his water.   _____

2. The little red __   _____   wagon   wanted   white
   carried the
   packages.   _____

3. That __ is very   _____   rivet   river   risen
   long and winding.
                        _____

4. He is going to __   _____   vent   viper   visit
   his granddad.
                        _____

5. Have you __   _____   ever   every   even
   seen a beautiful
   sunset?   _____

6. After you __ your   _____   finally   finish   final
   breakfast, you
   should brush   _____
   your teeth.

7. They use the __   _____   cabin   remote   couple
   in the mountains
   when they go   _____
   skiing.

8. Some people __   _____   trained   trample   travel
   to a different
   country every   _____
   year.

© Harcourt

Name _____

Write the word that answers each question.

alphabet	tears	year	wrap	ear
elephant	knots	cheer	knee	laugh

1. What animal has a trunk? _____

2. What do you do when you are excited? _____

3. What do you do when you hear a funny joke? _____

4. What do you wipe from your eyes after you cry? _____

5. What do you do to a gift? _____

6. What are all the letters from **A** to **Z** called? _____

7. What can you make with rope? _____

8. What do you hear with? _____

9. What lasts for 12 months? _____

10. What is the part of your body where your leg bends? _____

© Harcourt

Review Consonant Digraphs: *kn, wr, gh, ph*;
r-Controlled Vowel *ear, eer* • Read and Write Words

Name _____

Circle the letters that stand for the vowel sound you hear in each word. Then write the word on the line.

1. ea oy oi	2. ea oy oi	3. ea oy oi
4. ea oy oi	5. ea oy oi	6. ea oy oi
7. ea oy oi	8. ea oy oi	9. ea oy oi

© Harcourt

Name _____

1. She had tears in her eyes.   _____

2. Next year he wants to go
   on a trip.   _____

3. She was finally able to steer
   her bike.   _____

4. Have you ever seen a movie
   about a deer?   _____

5. She wore sheer tights.   _____

6. We always enjoy being at
   the beach.   _____

7. Sometimes my brother
   annoys me.   _____

8. My mom spoils my dog.   _____

9. My dad likes to broil his meat.   _____

10. Have you ever eaten soybeans?   _____

© Harcourt

Name _____

1. You do this when
   you have a cold.   _____ call   cough   catch

2. If you are not behind,
   you are this.   _____ ahead   among   around

3. This rhymes with
   block and is
   something you do
   to get in.   _____ knit   know   knock

4. If you are a boy,
   your aunt calls
   you this.   _____ nephew   nearly   nightly

5. This is the opposite
   of **right**.   _____ write   wrong   wren

6. When something
   is funny, you do this. _____ laugh   listen   learn

7. This is something
   you hang on a door.   _____ wrench   wreath   wrist

8. You might get down
   on this when you
   need to find
   something.   _____ knot   knob   knee

9. You might do this
   on a hot day.   _____ spread   sweat   spend

10. These are the
    letters **A** to **Z**. _____ autograph ahead   alphabet

© Harcourt

Review Consonant Digraphs: kn, wr, gh, ph;
Short Vowel: /e/ ea • Read and Write Words

Name _____

Write the missing letters to name each picture. Then write the word on the line.

1 _____ight	2 t_____s	3 d_____
4 g_____s	5 _____one	6 b_____l
7 br_____d	8 _____ist	9 thr_____d

Review Short Vowel: /e/ ea; Vowel Diphthongs: oi, oy; Consonant
Digraphs: kn, wr, gh, ph; r-Controlled Vowel: ear, eer • Read Words

© Harcourt

Name _____

Circle the letters that complete the word in each sentence. Then write the word on the line.

1. I always enj____ going to the farm. _____   oi   oy   ea

2. I like to help make the br____d. _____   oi   oy   ea

3. When I h____ the pigs oink, I giggle. _____   ea   ear   eer

4. Even the moo of the cows makes me lau____. _____   ph   gh   kn

5. I ____ow Grandpa wants to show me how to plant beans. _____   ph   gh   kn

6. We plow the s____l and put in the seeds. _____   oi   oy   ea

7. I try to be careful not to ____eck the crop. _____   ph   kn   wr

8. Before I leave for home, we take a ____oto to remember my time there. _____   ph   kn   wr

Review Short Vowel: /e/ ea; Vowel Diphthongs: oi, oy; Consonant Digraphs: kn, wr, gh, ph; r-Controlled Vowel: ear, eer • Read and Write Words

Phonics Practice Book

© Harcourt

Name _____

Help the  find its home. Color each picture whose name has the sound you hear at the beginning of 🦉 and in the middle of ☁️.

Vowel Diphthongs: *ou, ow* • Read Words

Name _____

The letters **ow** or **ou** can stand for the vowel sound you hear in **owl** and **house**. Write the word that names each picture.

<u>ow</u>l h<u>ou</u>se

hound   clouds   crown   cow   mouse   clown

1	2	3
_____	_____	_____

4	5	6
_____	_____	_____

Write each picture name from above in the correct column.

<u>ow</u>l

_____

_____

_____

h<u>ou</u>se

_____

_____

_____

© Harcourt

Vowel Diphthongs: *ou, ow* • Read and Write Words

Phonics Practice Book

Name _____

howl	crowd	sound	town	clouds
ground	clowns	growl	round	crown

1. One day, the king was in _____.

2. A very big _____ came to see him.

3. Everybody was on the _____ in the grass.

4. Big _____ were in the sky.

5. The king had a big _____ on his head.

6. It was _____.

7. It had pictures of happy, dancing _____ on it.

8. My dog started to _____.

9. The king must have liked the _____ because he started to bark.

10. That made the rest of us laugh and _____.

© Harcourt

Name _____

Read the poem. Then complete the sentences.

I want to be a funny clown
Who likes to jump up and down.
I'd have a nose that is red and
    round.
I'd stand on my hands to walk on
    the ground.

I'd paint on a smile, never a frown.
And every time I was in town,
I'd do my tricks in front of a crowd.
All the people would laugh out loud!

1. This _____ would be funny.

2. The red nose would be _____.

3. The mouth would not have a _____.

4. People in the _____ would laugh out loud.

Vowel Diphthongs: *ou, ow* • Read and Write Words   Phonics Practice Book

Name _____

An **abbreviation** is a short way to write a word. An abbreviation begins with a capital letter and ends with a period.

Thursday = Thurs.   January = Jan.   Doctor = Dr.   Road = Rd.

Circle the correct abbreviation for each word. Then write the abbreviation on the line.

1 March Mar mar Mar. _____	**2** Doctor dr. doc. Dr. _____	**3** Street Str. St. st. _____
4 December Dec. Decem dec _____	**5** Tuesday Tu. Tues. Tus. _____	**6** Avenue ave. av. Ave. _____
7 Saturday Sa. Sat. Satur. _____	**8** Road Ro. Ra. Rd. _____	**9** United States US u.s. U.S. _____
10 February Feb. feb. Febr. _____	**11** Wednesday Wed Wed. Weday. _____	**12** August Aug. Ast. aug. _____

© Harcourt

Name _____

1 Sunday _____	2 Monday _____
3 Friday _____	4 Saturday _____
5 April _____	6 September _____
7 October _____	8 November _____
9 December _____	10 United States _____

Rewrite each abbreviation correctly.

11 sept 12 _____	12 tues. _____
13 feb. 27 _____	14 Sat _____
15 Third st _____	16 jan 3 _____
17 mr. Jones _____	18 Sixth ave _____
19 Pine rd _____	20 Mrs Santos _____

Abbreviations • Read and Write Words

Phonics Practice Book

© Harcourt

Name _____

 h**orn**   c**ore**   f**our**

Write the word that names each picture.

snore   pour   fourth   corn   store
shore   horse   court   fork

1. _____

2. _____

3. _____

4. _____

5. _____

6. _____

7. _____

8. _____

9. _____

© Harcourt

Name _____

1. I am something to eat that rhymes with **born**.

   What am I? _____

2. Some people do this when they sleep. I rhyme with **bore**.

   What am I? _____

3. I come after three and rhyme with **pour**.

   What am I? _____

4. I am found on some bottles. I rhyme with **fork**.

   What am I? _____

5. I am a place where a judge is found. I rhyme with **fort**.

   What am I? _____

6. I am something you blow and rhyme with **worn**.

   What am I? _____

7. I tell where you shop and rhyme with **core**.

   What am I? _____

8. I am what you want when you have not had enough.

   I rhyme with **shore**. What am I? _____

© Harcourt

Name _____

Circle the letters that complete the picture name. Write the letters on the line.

1. or / ore / our st _____	2. or / ore / our c _____ n	3. or / ore / our c _____ d
4. or / ore / our h _____ se	5. or / ore / our sn _____	6. or / ore / our p _____
7. or / ore / our st _____ m	8. or / ore / our f _____ th	9. or / ore / our c _____ t
10. or / ore / our sh _____	11. or / ore / our f _____	12. or / ore / our st _____ k

© Harcourt

Name _____

Circle 10 words with **or**, **ore**, or **our** hidden in the puzzle.
Some words go across. Some words go down.

```
F  O  U  R  T  H  O  R  C
O  H  P  L  O  P  T  S  O
R  M  O  A  R  O  H  T  R
K  U  R  O  N  U  O  O  E
C  O  U  R  T  R  R  R  O
S  N  O  R  E  U  N  E  U
```

Write a word from the puzzle to name each picture.

1	2	3	4
_____	_____	_____	_____

5	6	7	8
_____	_____	_____	_____

r-Controlled Vowels: *or, ore, our* • Read and Write Words

Phonics Practice Book

© Harcourt

Name _____

For two-syllable words that have a single consonant between two vowels, the word is usually divided before the consonant if the first vowel is long.

pony   **po - ny**

v   cv

For two-syllable words that have a single consonant between two vowels, the word is usually divided after the consonant if the first vowel is short.

visit   **vis - it**

vc   v

Write each word, dividing it into syllables.

1 finish _____	2 frozen _____
3 paper _____	4 lady _____
5 clever _____	6 model _____
7 music _____	8 travel _____
9 lilac _____	10 river _____
11 wagon _____	12 broken _____

© Harcourt

Name _____

Last year my parents, brother, sister, and I went to the Grand Canyon. We stayed in a cabin ten minutes from the entrance. Since the Grand Canyon is huge, we planned to visit the park for four days. On our first day, we flew above the canyon. Our pilot showed us the different parts of the canyon. From so high in the air, the canyon did not look tiny. On the second and third days, we rode mules to explore the canyon. One night, we slept under the open sky. On the fourth day, we hiked and took pictures of all the great moments and sights. This famous place is great to travel to.

1 _____	2 _____	3 _____
4 _____	5 _____	6 _____
7 _____	8 _____	9 _____
10 _____	11 _____	12 _____

© Harcourt

Name _____

The letters **ew, ue,** and **oo** can stand for the vowel sound you hear in **new, true,** and **zoo**. Write the word that best completes each sentence.

stew	chewed	clue	flew
blue	school	cool	threw

1. I got my dog, Woof, at the end of the _____ year.

2. He is very _____, but he always gets into trouble.

3. Once he found my _____ socks.

4. He _____ them until they were full of holes.

5. Another time I _____ my ball to him.

6. He _____ after it and got it.

7. I don't have a _____ where he hid it!

8. Then there was that _____ that my mother cooked. It's a good thing that we love Woof!

© Harcourt

Name _____

The letters **ou** and **ui** can stand for the vowel sound you hear in **you** and **suit**.
Write the word that completes each sentence.

you

suit

youth	**juice**	**soup**	**group**
you	**fruit**	**suit**	**bruise**

1. Another word for *child is* _____ .

2. A word that rhymes with *do* is _____ .

3. Something good to drink is _____ .

4. Something hot and good to eat on a cold day
   is _____ .

5. If three children work together, they are in the
   same _____ .

6. If you fall, you can get a _____ .

7. Pants and a jacket that go together are
   a _____ .

8. An apple is one kind of _____ .

Vowel Diphthongs: *oo, ew, ue, ui, ou* • Read and Write Words

Phonics Practice Book

© Harcourt

Name _____

1. Find the juice. Put a glass under it.
2. Do you see the soup bowl? Color it green
3. Can you find the stool? Add two legs to it.
4. Find a plate, fork, and knife. Put a spoon next to the knife.
5. It is noon. Draw hands that point to 12 on the clock.
6. Do you see some fruit? Color it purple.
7. Can you find a pot of stew on the stove? Draw some steam over it.
8. Find the name of the month. Circle it.

© Harcourt

Name _____

Look at each picture. Then write the answer to each question.

1	Is this a clue or clay?	_____
2	Do people eat soap or soup?	_____
3	Are these boats or boots?	_____
4	Does she eat stew or stoop?	_____
5	Are they in a grape or a group?	_____
6	Is an apple a fruit or a foot?	_____
7	Do you sit on a stool or a steel?	_____
8	Would someone wear a seat or a suit?	_____
9	Is glue or glide sticky?	_____

Vowel Diphthongs: *oo, ew, ue, ui, ou* • Read and Write Words

Phonics Practice Book

© Harcourt

Name _____

A prefix is added to the beginning of a root word to make a new word with a different meaning.

mis = bad or wrong
re = again
un = not

Write the word with **mis, re,** or **un** that matches each meaning.

1 not true _____	2 tell again _____	3 not happy _____
4 behave badly _____	5 build again _____	6 lead in wrong direction _____
7 read with a wrong meaning _____	8 write again _____	9 not kind _____
10 fits badly _____	11 not safe _____	12 fill again _____

Name _____

1. If you are doubtful or not <u>certain</u> of something, then

   you are _____.

2. If you <u>do</u> something over again, you _____ it.

3. If you have wrong <u>information</u>, then you have

   _____.

4. If you <u>spell</u> a word wrongly, then you _____ it.

5. If you <u>create</u> something over again, you

   _____ it.

6. If an animal is rare or not <u>common</u>, it is

   _____.

7. If you <u>take</u> something over, you _____ it.

8. If something is put in the wrong <u>place</u>,

   it is _____.

9. If someone shows ill will or is not <u>friendly</u>, that person is

   _____.

10. If you <u>play</u> a game over, you _____ it.

© Harcourt

Name _JEFF HARDY_

A+

 ch**air**    m**are**

The letters **air** and **are** sometimes stand for the vowel sound you hear in **chair** and **mare**. Circle the name of each picture. Then write the word on the line.

1	shares / starts / _stairs_
2	mare / mint / main
3	hair / hare / hire
4	square / spray / spare
5	cheer / chore / _chair_
6	pear / part / pair
7	air / are / and
8	hold / harm / hair
9	bear / bare / barn

© Harcourt

Name _____

| chair | pair | hair | air | fair |
| share | stairs | square | mare | scare |

1	If you have two matching socks, you have this.	2	I grow on your head.
	_____		_____
3	I am what you breathe.	4	I mean "to make someone afraid."
	_____		_____
5	I am a place with rides to go on and prizes to win.	6	I mean "to take turns."
	_____		_____
7	I am a shape.	8	I am something you go up and down.
	_____		_____
9	I am a horse.	10	I am something to sit on.
	_____		_____

© Harcourt

Name _____

© Harcourt

Read each sentence and circle the word that has the vowel sound you hear in **chair** and **mare**.

1. Tim bought a pair of tickets for the show.

2. He wanted to have a spare ticket to give to a friend.

3. He knew the tickets were rare.

4. Tim told his friend Matt that he would share the ticket.

5. To be fair, Matt wanted to pay for the ticket.

6. Tim did not care about the money.

7. To get ready for the show, the boys combed their hair.

8. Then they walked down the stairs and went to the show.

Write the words you circled in the correct boxes below.

air	are

Name _____

Circle the sentence that tells about the picture.

1		The mare holds the pair of socks. The mare wears the pair of socks. The mare tears the pair of socks.
2		Clare draws a circle. Clare draws a tree. Clare draws a square.
3		The hare stands on its ears. The hare has one ear up. The hare sees a bear's eyes.
4		The bear sits on the stairs. The bear steers the car. The bear is at the steering wheel.
5		Blair sleeps in the chair. Blair is in the square. Blair gets up and cheers.
6		The colt is near the mat. The colt is near a bear. The colt is near the mare.

© Harcourt

r-Controlled Vowels: *air, are* • Read and Write Words

Phonics Practice Book

Name _____

A **contraction** stands for two words. An **apostrophe** takes the place of the letter or letters that were left out.
Write the contraction for the two words below each sentence.

she + is = she's

1. _____ not very big.
   I am

2. Look at my ears. _____ big!
   They are

3. Do you see my tail? _____ round.
   It is

4. Move the way I do. _____ hopping!
   You are

5. _____ hop away together.
   Let us

6. _____ going to have fun!
   We are

Draw a picture of the animal who is talking.

© Harcourt

Name _____

Circle the contraction that stands for the underlined words.

1. I <u>can not</u> wait until my grandma comes.	haven't can't don't
2. <u>She will</u> be here soon.	She'd She'll She's
3. <u>It is</u> her birthday.	I'm It'll It's
4. <u>We are</u> having a surprise party for her.	We'll We're We've
5. <u>I have</u> made her a big birthday cake.	I'd I'll I've
6. <u>Let us</u> go outside and wait for Grandma.	I'll He's Let's
7. <u>We will</u> hide and yell "Surprise."	We've We'll We'd

Contractions • Read and Write Words

Phonics Practice Book

© Harcourt

Name _____

Look at each picture. Then write the word that answers the question.

1		Is this a group or a gown? _____
2		Are these pairs or stairs? _____
3		Is this a deer or a mare? _____
4		Is she eating fruit or stew? _____
5		Is this a spear or a square? _____
6		Is this glue or juice? _____
7		Is this a moon or a mood? _____
8		Are these grapes a fable or a fruit? _____
9		Is this a suit or soup? _____
10		Is this a table or a tool? _____

© Harcourt

Name _____

1. Find the horse. Color it brown.
2. Look for the cow. Give it another horn.
3. Find the animal eating the apple core. Circle the core.
4. Who might pounce on the mouse? Make an **X** on it.
5. What sound will the owl make? Make a cloud by the owl and write WHO in it.
6. Count four pigs. Add one more.
7. Find the house. Add a door to it.
8. Who tore her shirt on the thorn? Color her shorts blue.

152

© Harcourt

Name _____

true	round	grew	noon	smooth
shampoo	juice	vowels	blew	soup

1. What did the birthday girl do to the candles?

   _____

2. When do some people eat lunch? _____

3. What do you eat when it's cold or you are sick?

   _____

4. When something is not false, what is it?

   _____

5. What might you drink at breakfast? _____

6. What shape is a circle? _____

7. What are **a, e, i, o,** and **u**? _____

8. What is the opposite of **rough**? _____

9. When you get taller, what do people say you did?

   _____

10. What do you wash your hair with? _____

© Harcourt

Name _____

Write the words that belong in the chart. Then draw a picture for the last word you write in each column.

store	hair	pour	shore	pair
corn	tour	care	tore	stairs
score	hare	short	court	horse
square	fourth	air	snare	forty

air	are	our	ore	or

© Harcourt

Name _____

Circle the name of each picture.

1 	more mare month	**2** 	grow grape group	**3** 	threw three there
4 	store stare shore	**5** 	clouds clowns clears	**6** 	count court chart
7 	fought feared fruit	**8** 	bats boots bores	**9** 	fear far four
10 	corn core cord	**11** 	hard have hare	**12** 	moth mouse month
13 	clay cone clue	**14** 	carry cowboy cattle	**15** 	chair chore chirp

© Harcourt

Name _____

1. We went to a country __ .   far   fur   fair

2. We saw a very funny __ .   clown   corn   coin

3. He ran after a __ .   house   horse   head

4. Then the horse ran to __ .   town   tear   tent

5. It chased the clown __
   the tent.   asleep   afraid   around

6. We laughed at that __ clown.   flew   fool   flute

7. The funny man __ a funny hat.   were   wore   water

8. We heard a __ of birds
   singing.   grape   green   group

9. They __ out of his hat.   flew   floor   flies

10. The clown's __ was purple
    and green.   sauce   suit   soup

11. His nose was stuck on with __ .   gown   grown   glue

12. The clown hoped he would
    soon go on a __ .   torn   tour   tent

© Harcourt

Name _____

The letters **ou** in **could** and **oo** in **foot** stand for the same vowel sound. Write the word that names each picture.

hook   wood   brook   hood   wool   book

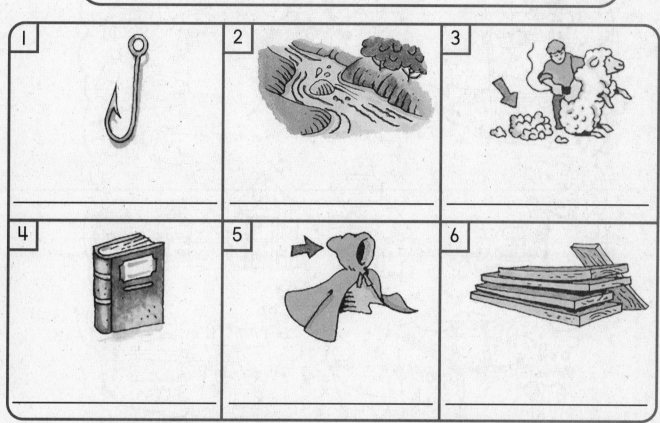

1. _____

2. _____

3. _____

4. _____

5. _____

6. _____

Write **yes** or **no** to each question. Then circle each word that has the same vowel sound you hear in **could** and **foot**.

7. Should you go swimming in a brook alone? _____

8. Would you bring a wool coat to the beach? _____

9. Could you cook while standing on one foot? _____

10. Should you wear a hood in the rain? _____

© Harcourt

Name _____

Do what the sentences tell you.

1. Find two children looking at a book. Color the book green.
2. Do you see a girl with a sheep? Make her stick look like a hook.
3. Who took a plum? Color the plum blue.
4. Which girl's bowl fell? Draw a circle around her.
5. One little pig makes his house of wood. Color the wood brown.
6. Who has a cape with a hood? Color the cape and hood red.
7. Who cooks? Color her dress purple.

© Harcourt

Name _____

```
C  S  H  O  U  L  D  K  W  T
O  T  A  B  W  O  O  L  O  W
U  O  H  O  H  O  O  K  U  O
L  O  C  O  O  K  R  C  L  O
D  D  U  K  F  O  O  T  D  D
W  B  R  O  O  K  H  O  O  D
```

Write a word from the puzzle to name each picture.

1	2	3	4
_____	_____	_____	_____

5	6	7	8
_____	_____	_____	_____

© Harcourt

Name _____

1	I wish that I ___ stay up late. _____	could cook cold
2	I would ___ up at the sky and study the stars. _____	lock lake look
3	I ___ draw pictures of what I saw. _____	world would worse
4	Then I would put them in a ___. _____	book brook brake
5	If I ___ my pictures to school, I would show them to my friends. _____	tool tone took
6	Everyone would say that they were very ___. _____	good gone gold
7	I ___ plan to stay up late tonight. _____	showed should shook
8	I will ask my ___ friends to come and watch the stars with me. _____	neither newspaper neighborhood

© Harcourt

Name _____

A **prefix** is added to the beginning of a root word to make a new word with a different meaning. Write the word with **dis, over,** or **pre** that matches each meaning.

dis = opposite of   **over** = above; too much of; past   **pre** = before

1	2	3
the opposite of loyal	to cook before	pay too much
_____	_____	_____

4	5	6
to view before	the opposite of agree	to plan before
_____	_____	_____

7	8	9
above one's head	to pay before	stay the night
_____	_____	_____

10	11	12
the opposite of comfort	the opposite of like	the opposite of obey
_____	_____	_____

13	14	15
the opposite of honest	too much heat	eat too much
_____	_____	_____

© Harcourt

Name _____

1. If you do not <u>agree</u> with your friend, then you

   _____.

2. If you are <u>charged</u> too much for something, you have been

   _____.

3. If you <u>cook</u> some of a meal ahead of time, then you

   _____ the food.

4. Something that <u>existed</u> before _____.

5. If you do not <u>approve</u> of something, then you

   _____.

6. If water <u>flows</u> over the banks of a river, the water

   _____.

7. If you do not <u>like</u> a certain food, then you

   _____ it.

8. If something is not <u>connected</u>, then it is

   _____.

9. If something is <u>rated</u> too highly, it is _____.

10. A <u>school</u> you go to before kindergarten is a

   _____.

© Harcourt

Name _____

dawn

The letters **aw** often stand for the vowel sound you hear in **dawn**. Write the letters **aw** to complete each picture name that has the same vowel sound as **dawn**. Then trace the whole word.

1	2	3
p___	cl___	tr___
4	**5**	**6**
str___	thr___	h___k
7	**8**	**9**
f___n	c___	y___n
10	**11**	**12**
f___n	s___	cr___l

Vowel Variants: aw, au(gh) • Write Words

© Harcourt

Write the word that answers each riddle.

1. I am an animal's foot, and I rhyme with *saw*. What am I? _____

2. I am part of your face. I rhyme with *law*. What am I? _____

3. I am what you are done to at school. I rhyme with *naught*. What am I? _____

4. I am what you do when you make a picture. I rhyme with *claw*. What am I? _____

5. I am the grass around a house. I rhyme with *yawn*. What am I? _____

6. I am a baby deer. I rhyme with *dawn*. What am I? _____

7. I am the girl child of my parents. What am I? _____

8. I am a bird that flies high. I rhyme with *squawk*. What am I? _____

© Harcourt

Vowel Variants: aw, au (gh) • Write Words

Name **Jeff HARDY**

caught   **dawn**

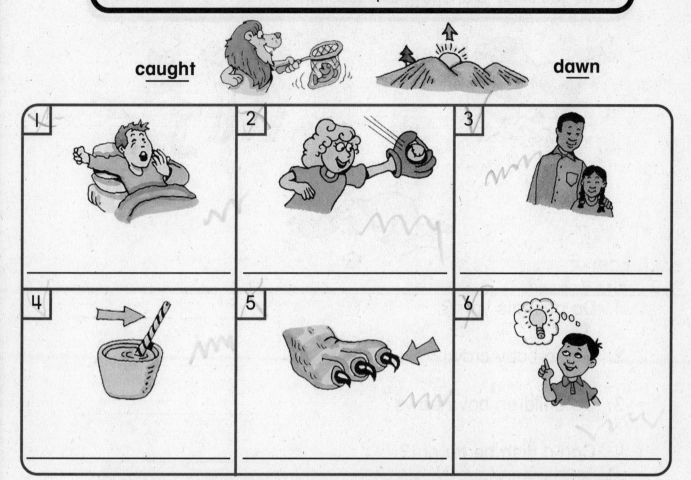

1.

2.

3.

4.

5.

6.

Circle the word that the sentence tells about.

7. If you saw one person reach for a ball, you could say the person did this.

    caught   coughed   crawled

8. If you are thirsty, you might take a drink and use this.

    string   straight   straw

9. If you are very tired, you might do this.

    yarn   yawn   yonder

10. When someone helped you learn to do something, he or she did this.

    treated   taught   tricked

© Harcourt

Name _____

1. Do animals yarn? _____

2. Can a baby crawl? _____

3. Do children have paws? _____

4. Can a dish be taught? _____

5. Can a daughter be a boy? _____

6. Do fawns have four legs? _____

7. Can hawks drink from straws? _____

8. Is a saw a sharp tool? _____

9. Should you have a lion on your lawn? _____

10. Can the dawn be caught? _____

© Harcourt

Name _____

Change **f** to **v** before adding **-es** or **-s**.
Change each underlined word to make it mean "more than one."
Write the word to complete each problem. Answer the problem.

wol<u>f</u>   **wol<u>ves</u>**   **kni<u>fe</u>**   **kni<u>ves</u>**

1. You have one <u>loaf</u> of bread. You get one more. How many

   _____ do you have? _____

2. Four _____ are eating. One <u>wolf</u> walks away.

   How many are left? _____

3. You eat one <u>half</u> of an apple. You eat one half more. How

   many _____ do you eat? _____

4. Five _____ are in the field. One <u>calf</u> joins

   them. How many are in the field now? _____

5. Six _____ are on the table. I take one <u>knife</u>

   away. How many are left on the table? _____

6. I found one <u>leaf</u>. My friend found nine more. How many

   _____ do we have? _____

© Harcourt

Phonics Practice Book   Endings: -es (f to v) • Read and Write Words   167

Name _____

1	knife	2	wife
	_____		_____
3	half	4	shelf
	_____		_____
5	life	6	leaf
	_____		_____
7	loaf	8	scarf
	_____		_____

Use a word from above to complete each sentence.

9. She has three _____ that she wears during the winter.

10. My brother keeps his toy cars on _____ in his closet.

11. I like reading about the _____ of famous people.

12. My family likes to see _____ during the fall.

13. They used sharp _____ to carve the pumpkin.

14. My mom made six _____ of pumpkin bread.

© Harcourt

Name _____

All the picture names end with **a(l).** Write the word that names each picture.

small	all	wall
hall	call	ball

1 _____

2 _____

3 _____

4 _____

5 _____

6 _____

Circle and write the word that completes each sentence.

7. When you return from the store, you can share what you

_____.

bring   bought   broke

8. If you had an idea, this would be a _____.

thought   taught   taunt

9. When you bring something from home to your friend's house, you can say you _____ it.

brought   brook   bought

10. If you feel that you should do something, then you

_____ to do it.

naught   sought   ought

Vowel Variants: *a(l), ough* • Read and Write Words

© Harcourt

Name_____

Write the word that best completes each sentence. Write the word on the line.

small	bought	brought	tall	mall
fall	sought	ought	thought	hall

1. Yesterday, my mom and I went to the _____ .

2. We wanted to buy some _____ clothes.

3. We _____ we might find some things at good prices.

4. I even _____ some money I had saved.

5. It was a _____ amount, but I could use it for something.

6. First, we _____ pants and shirts.

7. My mom _____ me two of each!

8. Then we went down the _____ to the shoes.

9. The pair I liked had heels that would make me feel _____ .

10. After that, my mom said that we _____ to head for home.

Vowel Variants: *a(l), ough* • Read and Write Words

Phonics Practice Book

© Harcourt

Name _____

The words below are in the puzzle. Some words go across. Some words go down. Circle each one.

small	ball	cough	fought	ought
call	thought	all	brought	wall

```
A  B  C  A  L  L  F  T  B
T  H  O  L  W  A  O  P  R
H  S  U  L  A  C  U  R  O
O  M  G  O  L  Y  G  W  U
U  A  H  U  L  C  H  P  G
G  L  A  G  C  D  T  J  H
H  L  M  H  N  T  T  W  T
T  R  P  T  B  A  L  L  D
```

Write each word under the correct heading.

Words with a(l)	Words with ough

© Harcourt

Name _____

1. It is something you should do.

   sought   fought   ought

2. This is something little.

   small   squall   tall

3. You can use a phone to do this.

   call   come   comb

4. When you are sick, you might do this.

   cook   could   cough

5. If you have an idea, you have this.

   thought   through   threw

6. If someone brings something, he or she did this.

   bright   brought   bought

7. If you are not short, you might be this.

   wall   tall   tell

8. If someone made a purchase, he or she did this.

   bought   bring   bright

9. When two people did not agree, they might have done this.

   finished   fraught   fought

© Harcourt

Name _____

A suffix is added at the end of a root word to form a new word.
tion means action; result of; being
connect = connection
Use the suffix **tion** to write a word to match each meaning.

1 act of connecting	2 act of constructing	3 condition of cooperating
_____	_____	_____
4 act of creating	5 act of correcting	6 act of rotating
_____	_____	_____
7 the process of acting	8 act of introducing	9 the act of inventing
_____	_____	_____

Use a word you just wrote to complete each sentence.

10. The workers began _____ on the building.

11. She wrote a very good _____ to her story.

12. There is a lot of fast _____ in that movie.

13. Bell's _____ of the telephone changed the world.

© Harcourt

Name _____

1 connection _____	2 perfection _____	3 completion _____
4 invention _____	5 suggestion _____	6 punctuation _____
7 protection _____	8 projection _____	9 action _____

Write a word to complete each sentence.

10. If you are being protected, then you have _____.

11. If you suggest something, then you have made a

    _____.

12. If you punctuate the end of a sentence with a period, you

    have used _____.

13. When you do something perfect, that is _____.

14. Something that a person invents is an _____.

15. When you connect things together, that is a _____.

© Harcourt

Name _____

The letters **ea, ei,** and **eigh** can stand for the long **a** sound you hear in **steak, veil,** and **eight**. Circle the name of each picture. Then write the word on the line.

steak   **veil**   **eight**

1	neither nearly neighbor	2	slide sleigh slip	3	weight wean when
4	stead still steak	5	rent reins risks	6	end eight either

_____

Write a word from above to complete each sentence.

7. My dad likes to have _____ and potatoes for dinner.

8. My next-door _____ likes to plant flowers in his garden.

9. My sister will be _____ on her next birthday.

10. The rider pulled tightly on the _____ to stop the horse.

© Harcourt

Name _____

weights	neigh	eight	break	weigh
sleigh	great	neighbor	steak	freight

1. When something is really good, it is this. _____

2. A type of train that carries a lot of goods is this. _____

3. This is the sound a horse makes. _____

4. This is something you can cook on a grill. _____

5. If you drop a dish, it may do this. _____

6. You can use a scale to do this. _____

7. This is someone who lives near your house. _____

8. People who work out lift these. _____

9. This is something you might ride in the snow. _____

10. This is the number between seven and nine. _____

© Harcourt

Name _____

1		great	weigh	sheep
2		break	sting	squeal
3		eaten	able	freight
4		when	great	wheel
5		steak	brand	braid

© Harcourt

Name _____

Circle the long **a** word in each sentence.

ea   **ei(gh)**

1. Look at the neighbor.

2. She has eight children.

3. Together they weigh 800 pounds.

4. Sometimes they go to the gym and lift weights.

5. They hardly ever eat steak.

6. Next year, they hope to go on vacation during spring break.

Write each word you circled. Circle the letters that stand for the long **a** sound. Then draw a picture for the word.

7	8	9
10	**11**	**12**

© Harcourt

Long Vowels: /ā/ *ea, ei(gh)* • Read and Write Words

Name _____

The suffixes **er** and **est** are added to root words to compare.
Sam is small. Mike is smaller than Sam. Ben is the smallest.
Add **er** and **est** to each word. Write the new words in the chart.

Word	Word + er	Word + est
1 nice	_____	_____
2 loud	_____	_____
3 kind	_____	_____
4 mean	_____	_____
5 dark	_____	_____
6 cool	_____	_____
7 tall	_____	_____
8 bright	_____	_____
9 new	_____	_____
10 dear	_____	_____

© Harcourt

Name _____

> Read the first sentence in each pair. Complete the second sentence by adding **er** or **est** to the underlined word.

1. Erin feels <u>cold</u>. Maxie is the _____ of everyone.

2. The apples are <u>fresh</u>. The oranges are _____.

3. It was <u>cool</u> last night. Tonight is even _____.

4. Her puppy is <u>cute</u>. My puppy is the _____ of all.

5. His room is <u>neat</u>. Her room is _____.

6. The cookies are <u>sweet</u>. The cupcakes are the _____ of the desserts.

7. That pillow is <u>soft</u>. This pillow is _____.

8. Nick's hair is <u>short</u>. Luke's hair is the _____.

9. Sean is <u>quick</u>. Nikki is _____.

10. That freight train is <u>slow</u>. This freight train is the _____ one.

Suffixes: *-er, -est* • Read and Write Words

Phonics Practice Book

© Harcourt

Name _____

haul   caught   bought

Write the word that completes each sentence.

because	caught	daughter	bought
brought	taught	ought	thought

1. Grandma _____ it would be fun to go fishing.

2. "I _____ to take Jenny along," said Grandma.

3. Jenny was Grandma's friend's _____ .

4. So Grandma _____ Jenny to the lake.

5. She _____ her how to fish.

6. Grandma said, "I am a good teacher, Jenny,
   _____ you did catch something!"

7. But all Jenny _____ was an old boot!

8. So Grandma and Jenny went to the store and
   _____ some fish for supper!

© Harcourt

Name _____

Choose the word that matches each clue. Write the word to complete the puzzle.

bought	fault	ought	squawk
claw	fought	sauce	taught
crawl	hawk	saw	thought

ACROSS
2. an idea
6. a chicken's sound
7. had a fight
9. paid for
10. to go on hands and knees

DOWN
1. should
3. a bird
4. did teach
5. a part of a cat's paw
6. something that goes on noodles
7. blame; mistake
8. a tool used for cutting

© Harcourt

Look at each picture. Then write the word that answers the question.

1		Has she crawled or caught it?	_____
2		Is this a paw or a paddle?	_____
3		Is this a bath or a brook?	_____
4		Would you hang clothes from a hook or a hood?	_____
5		Does he have a table or a thought?	_____
6		Does the number eight come before or after seven?	_____
7		Is this animal a fawn or a feather?	_____
8		Would you cut steak with a knife or a knock?	_____
9		Does a hammer or a hawk fly?	_____
10		Is she a dinner or a daughter?	_____

© Harcourt

Circle the sentence that tells about the picture.

1. Jimmy is having a great sleep.
   Jimmy is eight.
   Jimmy lifts weights.

2. The beaver bought a pretzel.
   The beaver taught the dog to gnaw.
   The beaver gnaws on the wood.

3. Heather is in a saddle.
   Heather is eating a steak.
   Heather skates on one foot.

4. Paul brought it to the stable.
   Paul has some sauce to eat.
   Paul drinks through a straw.

5. Dawn puts away a puzzle.
   Dawn steps around the pebble.
   Dawn saw too much paper.

6. Kate sits and uses a straw.
   Kate eats an apple on the lawn.
   Kate brought a flower ashore.

© Harcourt

Review *Vowel Variants; Long Vowel /a/* • Write Words

Phonics Practice Book

Name _____

1. The sky was sunny soon after d __ n.   _____   ough   aw   ea

2. It was going to be a gr __ t day.   _____   ea   ey   augh

3. I walked near the br __ k and into the woods.   _____   aw   oo   ough

4. A deer and her baby f __ n live there.   _____   ou   aw   ea

5. I th __ t I saw a bunny too.   _____   ea   augh   ough

6. I sh __ ld be careful not to scare the deer.   _____   ou   oo   ee

7. I c __ ld offer it some food.   _____   ou   oo   ee

8. I was glad that I had br __ t a cookie with me.   _____   ough   eigh   ey

9. I was able to br __ k it into small pieces.   _____   aw   oo   ea

10. I moved slowly bec __ se I did not want to scare the fawn.   _____   aw   au   ei

11. The deer just st __ d there and watched.   _____   ea   aw   oo

12. As I turned around, I c __ t sight of it eating the food.   _____   eigh   augh   aw

© Harcourt

Name _____

Circle the letters that complete each word. Then write the whole word.

1	ea / ey / (aw)	2	augh / ough / (eigh)	3	(al) / el / ea
4	(ough) / eigh / augh	5	oo / ou / ea	6	ea / ey / aw
7	(a) / augh / oo	8	(ough) / eigh / augh	9	ear / ar / (our)
10	a / (au) / aw	11	eigh / (ea) / ough	12	aw / ea / (oo)

Review *Vowel Variants; Long Vowel /ā/* • Read Words

Phonics Practice Book

© Harcourt

1

Popcorn

3

"Mmm, popcorn!" said Jen. "I like lots
of popcorn.
Let me pop some more."

Fold

Fold

8

"Come have popcorn, Ben," said
Red and Jen and Ted.
"MMM POPCORN!"

6

Pop! Pop! Pop! Pop!
"It will not stop," said Red.
"What can we do?" said Ted.

Pop! Pop! Pop!

Pop! Pop!

© Harcourt

Directions: Help your child cut and fold the book.
Phonics Practice Book

Cut-Out Fold-Up Book I • Short *o* Short *e*

187

"I have a pot. I will let it get hot. Popcorn will pop. Mmm, popcorn!" said Red.

— Fold —

"Mmm, popcorn!" said Ted. "It's not hot yet. I will drop some in. It will pop and pop."

— Fold —

"Get the pot!" said Red. "Get a mop!" said Ted. "Get help!" said Jen.

© Harcourt

Pop! Pop! Pop! "The pot is hot," said Red. "Come get popcorn."

pop! pop! pop!

Directions: Help your child cut and fold the book.
Phonics Practice Book

Tag and the Bug

© Harcourt

1

Snap! Tag snaps at the bug.
The bug gets away. It goes up.
Tag will get that bug.

Fold

Fold

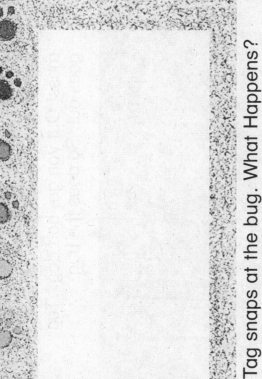

Tag snaps at the bug. What Happens?

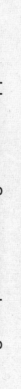

The bug is in here. Tag taps it.
He hits it. He rips it up.
Still no bug.

6

Directions: Help your child cut and fold the book.
Phonics Practice Book

Cut-Out Fold-Up Book 2 • Short *a*, Short *i*, Short *u*

189

Crash! Tag did not get the bug.
The bug lands on the lamp. Tag
still wants that bug.

The bug goes up and up.
It sees a hill.
It does not see the pup.

Fold

Fold

Tag jumps. The lamp tips and falls.
The bug falls to the rug. Tag will
get that bug.

"Stop, Tag," says Mom. "What a
mess! Out you go, bad dog." Tag
goes out. So does the bug.

© Harcourt

190 Cut-Out Fold-Up Book 2 • Short *a*, Short *i*, Short *u*

Directions: Help your child cut and fold the book.

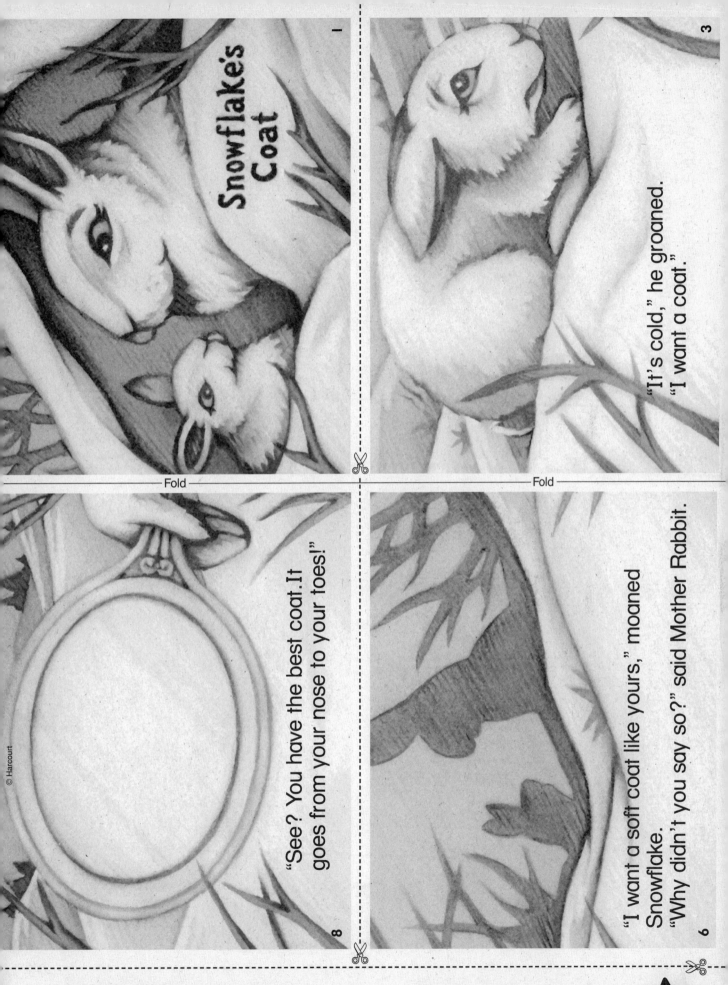

1

Snowflake's Coat

3

"It's cold," he groaned.
"I want a coat."

Fold

8

"See? You have the best coat. It goes from your nose to your toes!"

© Harcourt

Fold

6

"I want a soft coat like yours," moaned Snowflake.
"Why didn't you say so?" said Mother Rabbit.

Directions: Help your child cut and fold the book.
Phonics Practice Book

Cut-Out Fold-Up Book 3 • Long *a*, Long *o*

191

Mother Rabbit made a coat for
Snowflake. "Here, slip it on."

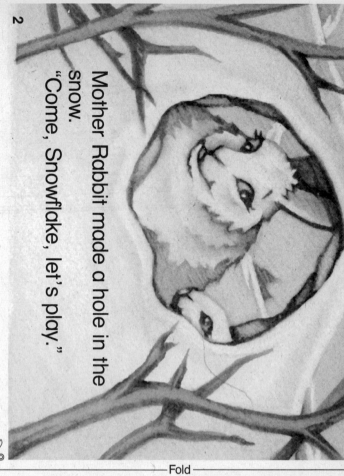

Mother Rabbit made a hole in the
snow.
"Come, Snowflake, let's play."

— Fold —

— Fold —

"This is too much coat," Snowflake
said.
"You'll grow," said Mother Rabbit.

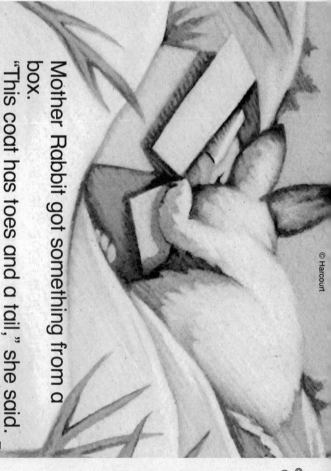

Mother Rabbit got something from a
box.
"This coat has toes and a tail," she said.

© Harcourt

Cut-Out Fold-up Book 3 • Long a, Long o

Directions: Help your child cut and fold the book.
Phonics Practice Book

The Bike Ride

1

Sheep said, "I need to rest. Let's sit next to this tree. It has pretty green leaves."

3

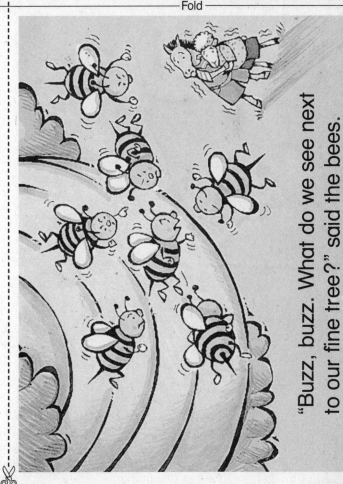

"Buzz, buzz. What do we see next to our fine tree?" said the bees.

6

© Harcourt

. . . Mule woke up. It was night. He put on the light. It had been a dream!

8

Fold

Fold

"Will you have a peach?" asked Mule.
"Yes, please. We can have tea, too," said
Sheep.

Sheep and Mule went on a bike
ride. They rode for five miles.

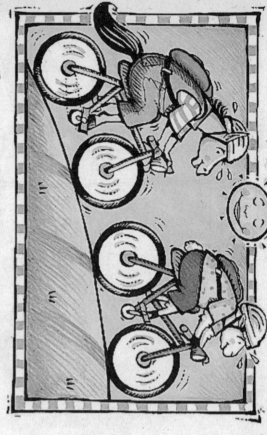

The bees dived down.
Mule and Sheep ran in fright.
Then . . . .

While Sheep
ate, Mule
jumped up.
"I see a big
hive," said Mule.

Cut-Out Fold-Up Book 4 • Long *i*, Long *e*, Long *u*

Directions: Help your child cut and fold the book.

© Harcourt

Fold

Fold

SHARKS

What are sharks like? Read to find out.

Fold

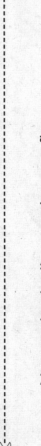

Sharks are born with sharp teeth. The little sharks can swim. Their mothers do not take care of them!

Fold

Sharks can live near and far from shore. They get air from the sea. That is because sharks are fish!

8

© Harcourt

Nurse sharks live on the sea floor. Carpet sharks do, too.

9

Some little sharks grow in "mermaid's purses." They grow inside these purses the way birds grow inside eggs.

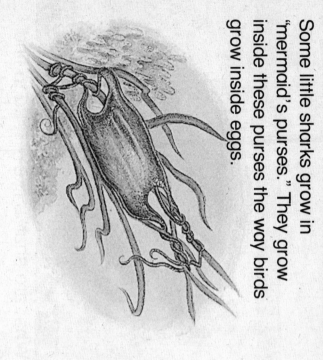

Some sharks will harm you. Other sharks will not.

Fold

Fold

You can see that sharks have sharp teeth. But you can not see their ears. The ears are inside.

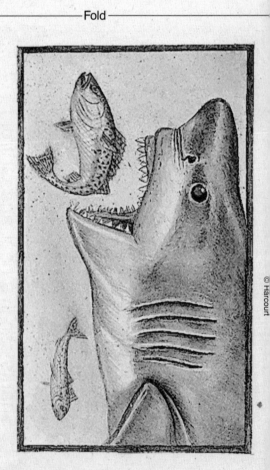

© Harcourt

The whale shark is so large that it might scare you. But do not fear! It will not hurt you.

5

7

196

Cut-Out Fold-Up Book 5 • R-Controlled Vowels

Directions: Help your child cut and fold the book.

A RIDDLE

1

I was round. I grew from the ground. My roots grew down for food. I grew and stood tall.

3

I gave you good clues. I taught you, too. Now draw me. Then show everyone what you drew!

8

I can be in a small group or in a big crowd, but I do not make a sound!

Directions: Help your child cut and fold the book.

Would you like to play a game? I will give you clues. Then you should know what I am!

2

Sometimes I am on a tree before the fruit grows.

— Fold —

I ought to make you smile, not frown. I can be a joy to see.

6

7

— Fold —

I can be brought inside. You can see me in a book or in a room.

© Harcourt

Directions: Help your child cut and fold the book.